APACHE COUNTRY

BUQUERQUE

FORT SUMNER

EW MEXICO

FORT STA

ESCALERO
SERVATION

DREAS
OUNTAINS

L PASO DEL NOR

RIO G

IN THE DAYS OF
VICTORIO

IN THE DAYS

James Kaywaykla, *narrator*

EVE BALL

ƆF VICTORIO

*Recollections of a
Warm Springs Apache*

 THE UNIVERSITY OF ARIZONA PRESS
Tucson, Arizona

About the Author . . .

EVE BALL has lived in the Ruidoso highlands of New Mexico, close to the Mescalero Reservation. Geography made her neighbor to the Apaches; sympathy and liking made her their friend; sensitivity to their part in the historic Southwestern drama made her their historian — able to see experience through their eyes, just as she used the lens of a pioneer Lincoln County woman to view and relate the saga of *Ma'am Jones of the Pecos* (UA Press, 1969).

About the Narrator . . .

JAMES KAYWAYKLA lived longer to recount Apache history than any of his fellow tribesmen. In his latter years, he often stayed in the author's home to unwind more continuously the thread of narrative. On the warpath in the 1880s with his chieftain elders, shipped with his people to Florida in 1886, Kaywaykla later was a member of a committee that selected Mescalero as the home of the Chiricahuas and the Warm Springs.

THE UNIVERSITY OF ARIZONA PRESS

Contents

ILLUSTRATIONS

MAPS

Foreword

We owe a debt of gratitude to Eve Ball for her history of the Warm Springs Apaches, as recalled by sons and daughters of the leaders of those Indians and narrated by James Kaywaykla. Eve's story is proof that she was kind and sympathetic and patient with the people who gave her the Indian version of occurrences pertaining to their tribe. An Indian does not tell every white man he meets the stories of his people.

And for good reason. I remember hearing my mother say: "If she keeps on nagging her old man she'll drive him to drink." At that time it was a puzzle. But now, years later, I know what she meant. That's what happened to our good Indians. White men — often a bunch of bums — abused the Indians and robbed them. Is it surprising they were frustrated and took to the bottle? Not all Americans have been honest enough to try to understand this.

Much has been written by the white man about the Apache: accounts have been written as military reports by young officers ambitious for promotion; reports have been compiled by Indian agents; by contemporary newspapers whose owners depended upon advertising paid for by merchants who lived by selling supplies to the reservations; by pioneers who entered country occupied and claimed by the Apaches, especially following the Civil War. Some of those stories were written by men who wanted to take over Apache country, but because of heroic resistance on the part of the

Apache were not immediately able to realize their objective. Seeking the support of public opinion, these intruders often pictured the Apache not only as warlike, but cruel and vicious — a people who should be driven from the mountains of the Southwest.

At best, the truths in these portrayals were only partial. At worst, they were no truths at all. The Indians have a philosophy of life in many ways better than what we have. How, for instance, can we compare our value of suffering with that of the Apaches? In the old days they trained their children to suffer because they knew suffering would come into every life. But that philosophy was not evaluated, nor was its existence even recognized in most of the white man's writing about the Apaches.

It is in the interest of historical accuracy to correct some of these erroneous or equivocal impressions by countering much that has been written. Eve Ball gives the Apaches' account of their history from 1878 to 1886. After the generation who related these events to Eve, the generation to follow can know little at first hand of the history of its people.

In 1916 I was assigned as a missionary of the Order of Franciscan Monks to the Mescalero Apaches. Three years before I arrived there, the Chiricahua Apaches, as well as some of the Warm Springs and the Nednhis, were brought to Mescalero Reservation to join the tribe and exercise equal rights with the Mescaleros. Night after night for many years I sat about their fires at their homes and listened to their stories. I heard from their own lips accounts given by descendants of Mangas Coloradas, Cochise, Victorio, Juh, Nana, Chihuahua, Naiche, Geronimo, Perico, Roman Grande, Big Mouth, Magoosh, Natzili, Gregorio, Sans Peur, Shanta Boy and many other Apaches — Chiricahua and Mescalero, Lipan and Jicarillo. In the main their stories were the same as those told to Eve Ball by James Kaywaykla and other informants.

Historians should welcome this opportunity to seek the truth on the side of the Apaches. Therein is the great value of Eve Ball's book, that she has presented the version of events most meaningful to the Apaches themselves.

FATHER ALBERT BRAUN, O. F. M.

Author's Preface

Fourteen years before I wrote the first word, I thought I was ready to begin writing about the Apaches. I had read the best source books and made the customary notes. History seemed to be a compilation of excerpts from various sources — good sources — joined together like beads on a string.

Though the Mescalero Apaches came to my hometown, the village of Ruidoso, New Mexico, to trade, nobody seemed to know much about them. The women trudged for miles with babies on their backs, and nobody asked them to ride.

I was told that each Indian on the Mescalero Apache Reservation received a check each month from the government. People believed this to be true, but I wanted to know. (It was not true.)

I found it very difficult to penetrate the wall of reserve behind which the Apaches kept themselves. I met Ramona Chihuahua Daklugie, wife of Asa Daklugie, and through her sought an interview with her husband. It was four years before he decided to talk to me. He was very influential among his people, and induced several of them to talk to me also.

When James Kaywaykla made his annual July visit to Mescalero for the Ceremonials for the Maidens, my Apache friends

[IX]

brought him to see me. Over a period of years following, he dictated to me his memories of the events of his childhood.

There were several men who could have been the narrator of the Apaches' story, for all of them were full participants in the turbulent history of the 1870s and 1880s. James Kaywaykla, perhaps because he lived longer than the others and perhaps because he lived away from the reservation and felt more freedom to speak, was able to spend the greatest amount of time in recounting to me the oral history of his people. Sometimes others also contributed accounts of their personal experiences or those of their fathers, among them Big Mouth (last living scout on the Mescalero Apache Reservation); Eugene Chihuahua (son of Chief Chihuahua); Jennie Chihuahua, wife of Eugene Chihuahua; Ramona Chihuahua Daklugie (daughter of Chief Chihuahua and wife of Daklugie); Ace Daklugie (son of the Nednhi chief, Juh and Geronimo's nephew and chosen successor); Isabel Perico Enjady, daughter of Perico (half-brother to Geronimo); Dahteste (widow of Scout Coonie); Hugh and Eliza Coonie, his children; Jasper Kanseah, nephew of Geronimo; Robert Geronimo, son of Geronimo; Dan Nicholas, son of a famous Chiricahua runner, Nicholas; his sister Minnie Zulega; Nelson Kedizhinne, cousin to Nicholas; Moses Loco, grandson of Chief Loco; Benedict Jozhe, grandson of Jozhe; George Martine, son of Scout Martine; Charlie Smith, who, with his mother, was captured by Geronimo's band and remained with them three years till sent to Florida; Willie Magoosh, son of Lipan Chief Magoosh; Solon Sombrero, grandson of Chief Natzili; Christian, Barnaby, and Amelia Naiche, children of Chief Naiche; Ralph Shanta, son of Shanta Boy; Lydia Shanta, daughter of Daklugie; Maude Geronimo, daughter of Daklugie; Alton Peso, son of Chief Peso; and Alton's sister, May Peso Second.

Some of these Apaches read the books I had valued so highly, and I was privileged to hear their reactions to the reports in those books. My books are filled with marginal notes in which the Apaches who had been present at various occurrences differed with the writers.

In these years I made a very sobering discovery: I knew almost nothing about Apaches. To know a people, one must be able to anticipate their reactions to certain circumstances. I learned that from James Kaywaykla.

"Which do you believe — me or that book?" he would ask.

"Both — especially if your accounts coincide," I assured him.

I used the best books written about the Apaches mostly for checking discrepancies among reports from witnesses of events which they related. I found many discrepancies.

In writing *this* book I am telling Kaywaykla's story. I have checked it with stories of other older members of the Warm Springs and Chiricahua bands, and have seen that even among themselves they differ in minor details. In chapter notes I have called some attention to various accounts to which they object. But this is Kaywaykla's story, and he had the support of his contemporaries in telling it. He accepted his grandmother's account of the occurrences at Tres Castillos, though he is informed as to conflicting records left by the officers and recorded by historians. He had no reason to believe, for example, that Chief Victorio was not an Apache; yet he respected the conflicting opinions of those who hold this in question.

After years of almost daily contact with these people I realize that I may still not be adequate for the task I have undertaken. I still do not understand them as one should who attempts to re-create their experiences and their injustices at the hands of my race. Yet I could not in my lifetime do them justice, nor in all probability could anyone else living who has the opportunity that I have had to hear their stories from their own lips.

It is my hope that this account of their sufferings may bring about sympathy and understanding among the children of their conquerors. These qualities have been lacking, but I sense a growing trend in our times toward realization of the wrongs the Apaches have endured. I feel hopeful that the U.S. government may — before the race is extinct — rectify some of them. As an example, for the reservations of which they were deprived — those of Cochise in Arizona and Victorio in New Mexico — no remuneration has been received, though claims for it have been in litigation for many years.

Of the Chiricahua and Warm Springs Apaches who went to Florida in 1886, only four were living by 1968, two on the Mescalero Apache Reservation — Eugene Chihuahua and Helen Chato, widow of the scout. There were two at Apache, Oklahoma — Mrs. Talbot Goody and Mrs. David Chinny, who died in 1969.

The Apaches were prisoners of war for twenty-seven years.

Their children were born in captivity; even many of their grand-children were born before the tribe was released. I have hoped to make the reader live their story with them — to see the Apaches' experiences through their eyes.

The narrator, James Kaywaykla, died in his sleep at Fort Sill, Oklahoma, June 27, 1963, at about 90 years of age.

EVE BALL

$\mathcal{A}$ Word From the Narrator

Until I was about ten years old I did not know that people died except by violence. That is because I am an Apache, a Warm Springs Apache, whose first vivid memories are of being driven from our reservation near Ojo Caliente with fire and sword.

As I tell this story, I am the sole survivor of the Massacre of Tres Castillos in which our great leader, Chief Victorio, fired his last bullet before taking his own life, and in which his band of almost four hundred people was nearly exterminated. Among the seventeen who escaped death or slavery were my mother and myself. She managed to make her way to Nana, a chief whom I will call Grandfather but white men would call my great uncle. It was Nana about whom the survivors assembled before making their desperate flight to the Sierra Madre. Our warriors were away on a raid for ammunition when the attack occurred, but later they joined Nana, a few at a time.

Victorio had killed many people, but the count was small in comparison to the number of lives Nana exacted in retaliation for Victorio's death. This was conceded at one time by Geronimo and also by Juh, a Nednhi chief, who terrorized southern Arizona for years.

From the time that we, as peaceful noncombatants, were driven from our reservation until we were herded aboard a train at Holbrook, Arizona, and shipped to Florida in 1886, we had been hunted through the forests and plains of our own land as though we were wild animals.

I have read widely and am familiar with the military reports about my people and with the records of the historians. Some of these records have been set down with sympathy and accuracy. I respect the historians' attempts to record the deeds of my people. These men, even as I am doing, have written either what they saw or were told by people on whose word they relied.

For twenty-seven years my people were prisoners of war. For several of those years I was a student at Carlisle Indian School in Pennsylvania. When I returned to my people they had been moved from Florida via Mount Vernon Barracks, Alabama, to Fort Sill, Oklahoma. Some of the older ones were dead, among them Nana. Kaytennae, my stepfather, had been Nana's companion for years, and had taken over his office as historian. Kaytennae, Mother, and Grandmother were teaching the young of our tribe the old stories and traditions.

I married Dorothy Naiche, daughter of the Chiricahua chief, Naiche, and therefore was closely associated with this leader for years. Chief Loco was my relative also, and I heard his version of events. I knew also Geronimo, who dictated his experiences to G. M. Barrett, with Asa Daklugie, son of Chief Juh, interpreting. Jason Betzinez, though a mature man, had been in Carlisle with me, as had Jasper Kanseah, and all of us sought to preserve the history of our peoples.

I say *peoples,* though the White Eyes designated the members of all four different Apache bands as Chiricahua. This was an error, for only the tribes of Cochise and Chihuahua were true Chiricahua. In our own tongue we are *Chihinne* — Red People. This does not refer to the color of our skins, but to a band of red clay drawn across our faces. Juh was chief of the *Nednhi* Apaches, whose stronghold was in the Sierra Madre of Mexico. Geronimo was leader, but not chief of the *Bedonkohes* whose territory was around the headwaters of the Gila. Though closely associated, we were distinct groups.

Of the Apaches taken to Florida, very few are living as I tell this story. On the Mescalero Apache Reservation in New Mexico there are three: Eugene Chihuahua, son of Chief Chihuahua, a Chiricahua; Helen Chato, widow of Scout Chato; and Sam Kenoi, son of Gordo, called "Fatty" by the White Eyes. At Apache, Oklahoma, are Talbot Goody and his wife, who was an infant when taken to Florida; David Chinny and his wife, and myself. All of us are advanced in years. All realize that we are not just ourselves facing the sunset, but the sunset of our race.*

All are still looking forward to the settlement of a claim against the government of the United States for reservations taken from the Chiricahua in 1876 and the Warm Springs in 1878. This debt is as yet unpaid. For many years my people have attempted to collect, but without results. I should like to see my government vindicated, though this possibility seems remote.

I have given Mrs. Ball what information I have concerning my people so that our descendants may know of the courage and resourcefulness of their ancestors. I hope, also, that this account may bring about a better understanding of the Apache among white Americans.

JAMES KAYWAYKLA

---

*The Apaches mentioned by Kaywaykla as living died before 1970.

IN THE DAYS OF
VICTORIO

Land of the Warm Springs Apaches

Flight

I was awakened by shots and I knew that it had come. Screams! More shots!

Entangled in my blanket I struggled to my feet. Grandmother lifted me to her shoulders and ran from our brush arbor on the east slope of the mountain. Above us a wickiup burst into flames as she ran toward the spring.

People on foot raced past us. A horse almost ran us down. There were flashes of fire and the whine of bullets. Grandmother stumbled across a body but regained her footing.

"Tight, tight, Torres,"* she muttered as she stooped to fill partially her water jug. Then she followed the soft thud of moccasins up the steep slope of the mesa. It seemed a long time before she reached the rim. Trembling with exhaustion she put me down and took my hand. We ran toward a clump of vegetation, and there she stopped to fold and arrange the blankets. She set out for another clump of mesquite; and from one to another we went.

As I trotted beside her I could see the faint glow of dawn before us. I tried hard to keep the pace. When I fell behind she lifted me again and did not stop until she reached the bank of a dry arroyo. She dropped me into the arroyo and we lay flat until we could

---

*As a boy, the narrator was called Torres until Chief Victorio gave him the name, Kaywaykla.

breathe easily. Then she set out, crawling on hands and knees, up the watercourse. I followed, moving when she did, stopping when she stopped. Creep and freeze! Creep and freeze! She'd taught me that game, and I'd played it with other children at Ojo Caliente [Warm Springs]. My hands touched damp sand, and I knew that some of the water had been spilled from the jug.

The arroyo bent sharply to the east and Grandmother stopped to listen before rounding the turn. I heard the hoofs of horses — shod horses — coming close. Then came the jingle of metal and the sound of harsh voices — White Eye voices. I lay still and held my breath. A horse snorted — he had smelled us! There was a long silence. Then I heard them plunge into the arroyo and scramble up the east bank. The sounds gradually died away, but we lay still for a long time.

Daylight was upon us before Grandmother resumed her crawling. She did not risk raising her head to look after the cavalry until we reached a place where the bank was well screened with cactus. The Blue Coats were still riding toward the Río Bravo [Río Grande]. She let me drink from the jug, and she gave me a handful of dried venison from the buckskin bag attached to her belt.

I, too, had a food bag, a small one containing mesquite bean meal. For months no Apache child had been without his emergency rations, nor had he slept without an admonition not to remove it, and not to abandon his blanket in case of attack. My food bag had never left me, day nor night.

"You're a good boy; you kept your blanket."

"Where's Siki?"* I asked.

"She left the village before we did. I had given her instructions long ago as to where to stop so that we can find her. I hope she remembers. If she obeys, the soldiers will not capture her."

"Why do they hunt us?"

"They have orders to kill every Apache, man, woman, or child, found off the reservation."

"But this is our reservation."

"It is no longer ours. The land Ussen created and gave to the Apache, is no longer ours. This, the land promised to Victorio by the Great Nantan in Washington, has been taken from us. He

*Daughter of Chief Loco, cousin of Kaywaykla.

promised it to our Chief and our people forever. And only two summers ago! Perhaps the gold for which the White Eyes grovel in the earth has been found in our mountains. Because of that the word of the Great White Chief means nothing. He has ordered that we go to San Carlos, the worst place in all Apachería, the vast land of our people. I have been to that place when Victorio took his people there. So many died that we fled from it and returned to Warm Springs. You, too, went, but you were too small to remember. Not many babies lived to return.

"Victorio will die fighting before he will permit the Warm Springs Apaches to be forced back to San Carlos again. Instead we go to the Great River where we meet those of us who escape.[1] Grandfather Nana will go to the three chiefs of the Mescaleros, our brothers, and ask for refuge on their reservation. He is to meet us at the river with horses and ammunition."

"Is it far to the river?"

"Not if we could stand and walk. Moving as we do it is perhaps three days."

I think it may have been mid-afternoon before we reached the head of the arroyo. We had a bare ridge to cross, one with little cover except occasional clumps of bear grass and scattered stones. We lay flat and wriggled from one cover to another until well over the crest. Several times Grandmother spied moving dots, and each time we lay motionless until she felt sure that the soldiers were still riding toward the east. She knew that with field glasses they might see us.

We made our way southeast until we reached the head of another dry stream bed leading to Cuchillo Canyon. We slipped between its protecting banks and worked our way south. There was a Mexican village in the canyon but Grandmother knew we had little to fear from it. The arroyo gradually became deep enough that Grandmother could stand and walk without fear of being seen. Toward dark we reached an overhanging rock. The encircling walls formed a sort of cave, open only on one side. She stopped and called softly. In the darkness something moved. She called again — a quail whistle — and a shadow stole toward us.

"Siki?"

"Yes, Grandmother, I waited as you told me."

"*Enjuh!* [Good!] I was afraid you might not find the place."

"I had no trouble. Grandmother, I'm hungry."

"So am I. So is Torres, but he has not asked for food. You had a bag. Where is it?"

"I took it from my belt to sleep."

"Torres did not. He obeyed. To obey is to live. And your blanket?"

"I was frightened —"

"So was I. So was Torres; but he held on to his blanket."

"I'm sorry, Grandmother."

"You're sorry! You know it is everyone for himself."

Siki crept from under the rock. "I'll go, Grandmother."

"You will not. Go back and sit down."

She took a handful of dried venison from her bag and mesquite meal from mine. She handed it to Siki. Then she filled my hand and took a small portion for herself. We ate. She bade Siki lie next to the wall, and me beside her. She spread both blankets over us and crept under the edge of them with her face to the open side. Knife in hand she slept.

Before dawn she had us on our way across a gentle slope toward another arroyo. Once within its banks we walked until Grandmother stopped to examine a trail sign. It was a row of little stones with a slightly larger one at the south end.

"A woman and children — seven in all. Too many! They should have separated so that each group might have a chance to live."

An hour or so later she found another message. Four had turned east; the rest kept on south.

"*Enjuh!*"

"Why?"

"The older children have struck out east to the river."

Until almost evening we moved cautiously. I was very thirsty but knew better than to ask for water. The jug was empty but Grandmother continued to carry it, for it requires much time and labor to weave a wicker jug and coat it with piñon gum so it will not leak.

We were nearing the Cuchillo. The arroyo was deep, with much vegetation along its banks, and we did not leave its shelter until dark. We walked cautiously, stopping often to listen and to sniff the air. I think I caught the tantalizing odor of meat as soon as Grandmother. Burning wood, too! I was cold as well as hungry. And thirsty! Grandmother murmured an order, and Siki and I sank to the ground. She was gone some time before we heard the quail call. Siki touched me. We waited for a second call before answering. Grandmother came with water and we drank.

"A sheep herder's camp, not a Mexican, but a White Eye. He has gone to Cuchillo, but it is not far. He may be back soon. Come!"

Flames flickered before the queer square tepee. The meat was suspended above them instead of being laid on coals in the proper manner. I dropped near the welcome fire while Grandmother and Siki went into the tent. In a very short time they returned with bundles wrapped in white cloth. Siki had a blanket and a knife. They cut the meat and each carried a piece.

In the shelter of the next arroyo we ate the partially cooked food. Grandmother cut long strips of meat. Mine she cut into small chunks, but she and Siki placed the ends in their mouths and deftly severed the bits with their knives. I was so hungry that I crammed two at a time into my mouth and chewed greedily.

"Not so fast, Torres. You must eat like a chief, for you come from a long line of them. You can never be one unless you practice self-control. A chief must have good manners."

I know that Nana never acted as though he were hungry, though he must often have been. I ate more slowly, enjoying every morsel of the good food. Then I stretched out on the ground and must have slept almost instantly. I awoke when Grandmother touched me.

"We must walk. Before day we must cross the big trail of the White Eyes in their journeys up and down the river."

"Are we close to the river?"

"About halfway between it and Cuchillo."

"Why does Grandfather say that Cuchillo Negro is a good name?"

"It is the name of Black Knife, a chief and our relative. And a black knife is not easily seen; that is why we darken the handles with clay."

Apaches do not like to travel by night, but Grandmother had no choice in the matter. When I became too weary to keep up she or Siki carried me. I did not know when they reached the river. I awoke in a mesquite thicket where a little group of our people was huddled. Siki rolled up in her blanket and slept, but Grand-mother went among them to check for the missing.

The next time I awoke Grandfather sat beside me rubbing his lame foot. His face was wrinkled and thin. His body was wrinkled and thin. He was tall, almost as tall as Naiche, who was the tallest of the Apaches. Nana was old, how old he did not know. In our tongue he was called Broken Foot, but never in his presence. It was rude to name one in his hearing; and when necessary to refer to him, it was customary to call him Nantan or leader. To tell the story, however, I call my people by name; it was not our custom to do so. Nor did anyone mention Grandfather's infirmity in his presence. He asked no odds because of either age or lameness; and frail though he was, Nana was universally feared and respected for his fighting ability.

When I looked into his shrewd old eyes he smiled and drew me into the embrace that is the greeting between men of our tribe. Then strong hands lifted me and I was enfolded in the arms of my father. My mother, Gouyan [Wise Woman], next embraced but did not kiss me, for that was an intimacy abhorrent to Apaches.

I had seen little of my parents, for my father was a brave war-rior, and my mother's place was at his side. She prepared food, dressed wounds, and when necessary fought beside him as bravely as any man. She, like all Apache wives, spaced her children about four years apart, and as soon as a baby could be separated from her, turned it over to the care of its grandmother.

I asked for my grandmother. Mother smiled and reminded me that she could not come to us because of my father's presence. I saw her standing some distance away, with her back to us. "I want Grandmother," I said.

"Then go to her," replied Mother. "It is natural that you love her best of the family. She has taken care of you since you were a baby."

"Gouyan, your name fits you well. You are intelligent with reason. You understand why the boy loves his grandmother," said my father.

Riders with many horses were entering the thicket. My par-ents joined them as they dismounted. My father led two mounts apart and Grandmother obeyed his summons to join him.

"You came by the camp from which we fled?"

"Yes, my sister. We buried the dead; fortunately there were few: the Lame One, two women, and the entire family camped on the hill above you. They camped apart for protection of the larger group and gave their lives that you might escape. We recovered many of the horses stampeded by the cavalry. And we captured many of theirs — enough, I think, to mount all who made it here. The river is rising rapidly and in a short time it may be impossible to cross. Prepare to ride."

From the stores brought in by the warriors, people hastily filled their individual food bags. They divided ammunition, rolled blankets, and tied them to saddles. My grandmother mounted a cavalry horse and Nana lifted me to a seat behind her. He took a buckskin thong and tied my belt firmly to hers. He saw that the blankets were secure and turned the horse to the water's edge. Siki, astride another, followed.

"Where's Mother?" I asked.

"She rides with your father and Nana on another raid."

The long line of horses faced the current. The women began to sing the Prayer to the Great River. It was accompanied by the ululating sound produced by tapping the hand over the open mouth. This prayer had long been used by my people to secure a safe crossing when the river was in flood. As the singing ended I saw flashes of turquoise as pieces were tossed into the angry water. That was the signal to plunge into the stream, but nobody moved. Then Blanco, my father's brother, rode along the line urging first one and then another to ride into the torrent. He was a medicine man, with great Power, but they did not obey. I heard him chide them: "When there is no danger you forget Ussen, but when you fear for your lives you pray to Him. You pay little heed when I tell you how to live; but when you face death you remember your religion. Songs and prayers avail little to those who have not lived according to the will of Ussen. You are in much greater danger from the cavalry on your trail than from the river. Is there no brave woman who will take the lead?"

Grandmother urged her mount to the brink and tried to force him to take the plunge. There was a commotion and the long line parted to let a rider through. I saw a magnificent woman on a beautiful black horse — Lozen, sister of Victorio. Lozen, the woman warrior![2] High above her head she held her rifle. There was a glitter as her right foot lifted and struck the shoulder of her horse. He reared, then plunged into the torrent. She turned his head upstream, and he began swimming.

Grandmother called to Siki to follow as cold water splashed into my face. She bent forward, and so did I. Water tugged at my feet and then my waist. When it washed over my shoulders I clung to Grandmother. My head went under, and then lifted above the water. The horse swam steadily across the broad stream until he found footing. His forelegs lifted and he scrambled onto a hidden ledge and waded ashore. I kept my seat until he began shaking himself; then I began slipping until Grandmother pushed me back in place.

Horses were floundering in the shallow water and coming ashore. One had washed down stream with its rider until Lozen overtook it and got it up the bank. When Lozen joined us, people had dismounted and begun to wring the water out of clothing and blankets.

Lozen came straight to Grandmother.

"You take charge now. I must return to the warriors. Head for the Sacred Mountain in the San Andres, and permit only short stops until you reach it. Camp near the spring and wait there until Nana comes. We can spare no men, but the young boys will obey your orders. Nana has told them that you are in charge. Get the people mounted and start. I go to join my brother."

Grandmother told the half-grown lads that theirs was the most dangerous of all positions, that of rear guard.

Then she led the way, with the long line following.

Refuge

Salinas Peak, the highest in the San Andres Range, is our Sacred Mountain. To it our medicine men go, not only for herbs, but for that far more efficacious instrument of healing which we call Power. Just what Power is I cannot explain, for it is beyond my comprehension. Those who seek it go alone that they may be tested for worthiness. It is a gift to be bestowed not only for virtue but for prayer and courage. If the applicant bravely endures hunger, fear, and other tests of which we do not speak, he may receive a healing art, usually for some specific illness. Or he may be given the ability to do some seemingly impossible things such as the Power possessed by Lozen.

When Victorio wished to know the location of the enemy, Lozen stood with outstretched arms, palms up, and prayed to Ussen. As she turned slowly, following the sun, her hands tingled and the palms changed color when they pointed toward the foe. The intensity of the sensation indicated the approximate distance of the enemy. The closer the adversary, the more vivid the feeling. Time after time I have seen her stand thus to ascertain the direction and proximity of the pursuers. I have always believed, along with many other Apaches, that had Lozen been with us at Tres Castillos her brother would never have ridden into the trap of the Mexican cavalry.

Nana said we crossed into Mexico during the Indian Moon —
September; it was at that time that Apaches and Comanches raided
for horses. Sánchez knew well the customs of Mexicans; so did
Victorio. Where the Indians met with no resistance they took little
plunder. If cattle or horses were conveniently left in corrals some
distance from the houses, the inhabitants were not disturbed. And
never did we take all the herds. We did not care much for cattle, and
we took care to leave enough horses so that the Mexicans could raise
more for us.

It was perhaps much later that scouts reported to the chief that
there was unusual activity at Carrizal — much coming of men and
talking in the plaza. Sánchez volunteered to go to the village and
learn the cause. He had killed a *vaquero* [Mexican cowboy] near
the Río Grande and kept the costume. He donned it, mounted a
horse bearing the Terrazas brand, and rode boldly into the village.
He walked leisurely about, had a drink at the *cantina,* and talked
with *mozos* [servants] in the plaza. He learned of a plan to invite
Victorio and his men to the settlement, ply them with liquor, and
kill them. Sánchez visited with other *vaqueros* and rode out un-
challenged. A day or so later a Tarahumara Indian came to camp
with an invitation for our men to visit Carrizal. The chief received
him courteously and thanked him, and ordered that the man be
permitted to return safely to the village.

Many of our men were away on a raid for ammunition. That
was good. The Tarahumara would report a small force. The raiders
returned with good horses, and at first the chief was pleased. But
when Sánchez saw the brand he shook his head. It was that of
Terrazas, Big Chief of the City of Mules, and he would surely exact
revenge. Well, let him come. He would not find the Apaches asleep.
The chief selected his ambush, concealed the women and children
on a mesa above the canyon, stationed his men, and waited.

There was much vegetation up on the mesa and especially along
the rim. It afforded fine concealment for those watching the canyon.
At our backs there was an arroyo for concealing the horses, which
were kept saddled. Beyond the mesa was a long gradual slope to the
south offering easy retreat. As usual, sentinels were posted in all
directions. Grandmother took her place on the edge overlooking
Nana's men. At points commanding the mouth of the canyon, men
were stationed to signal if the enemy approached from the west.

The sentinels were provided with bits of mirrors to flash warn-
ings. When General Miles wrote of his campaign against the Apaches
he assumed that we knew nothing of the heliograph. He was mistaken.
My people did not know the Morse code, but they had learned that
mirror flashes warned soldiers and ranchers of our movements; and
they, too, made use of the device. I've often wondered why so much
has been written about smoke signals. As far as I know they were
not much used.

On the north slope of the canyon, overlooking the little stream,
Victorio stationed a few picked men. Nana led another few up the
south slope and placed them behind boulders. Victorio stayed on
the mesa with us until warning flashes from the points of entrance
indicated the approach of the enemy. He lay on the rimrock, peering
through field glasses, the first I had seen.

"Mexicans, but not cavalry," he said. And he took his men and
joined Nana. Siki, Mother, and Blanco's wife checked the horses,
tied their equipment to the saddles, and hobbled their mounts.
Mother was the first to spy the riders, tiny specks moving toward the
canyon. Slowly they increased in size and rode single file up the
little stream. They dismounted, drank, watered their horses, and then
rode straight into our ambush. Kaytennae let every man pass the
boulder behind which he lay before opening fire. Those on the left
killed every horse before starting on the men. Two of the twelve fell,
as the Mexicans retreated up the south slope where Nana's forces
were hidden. It was over very quickly. The warriors walked among
the bodies collecting rifles and ammunition belts. A body moved and
was impaled on a spear. The warriors took shirts and saddles, and
toiled up the slope to the mesa.

The men were not tortured; the bodies were not mutilated. I
know, for I lay on my belly and watched this thing happen. I have
seen hundreds killed, none tortured. Mutilation that has occurred
was done after death, and that for the purpose of avenging mutilation
perpetrated on the body of Mangas Coloradas. Nor did Victorio's
band scalp. I never saw a scalp taken, and I was with his band until
he died. Why were these things told?

The chief came, but did not give the order to mount. We remained in camp. There was not even a victory dance though many
of the young men wanted one. We remained as we had been with
guards posted. When the young men divided the spoils, Victorio

withdrew. When he came to Grandmother's place for his food he hardly spoke. He seemed depressed, and not even Nana asked questions.

Grandmother said, "He grieves for his wife and little son, Istee, whom he left in the Black Range. The wrongs suffered by his people depress him. Who is there among us who has not cause for unhappiness?"

"Yet I am glad we have Lozen," said Mother. No other has the Power of locating the enemy."

"Victorio's scout will attend to that."

"With only their eyes and ears to help them. Lozen's Power surpasses that."

"Where is Lozen's husband?" I asked.

"She has no husband. You are too young to understand. She was a beautiful girl. When we made her feast, many young men wished to marry her. She refused all and Victorio would not compel her to choose."

"There are many women whose husbands are dead."

"But Lozen never married. When she was very young a strange thing happened. Warriors reported seeing one they called The Gray Ghost in our mountains. This one rode alone, and could never be approached. He was of great stature and very powerful. Once three warriors up on a point saw him pursued by cavalry into a canyon. They called to him and pointed out a secret hiding place. He nodded, rode into it, and stayed until the soldiers had given up the chase. He came to our camp and remained for some time, visiting with our people. He learned some of our words and told Victorio he was a chief from far toward the rising sun.

"A strange wagon came through our land. Twelve men rode beside it as guards. There was also a driver, and with them was an old woman. All spoke the language of Mexico, but they were not Mexicans. Inside the wagon they carried a young woman — very beautiful. When they moved west Gray Ghost followed.

"Lozen was too young for marriage, but she had seen this chief, and no other man ever interested her. She put marriage from her mind and rode beside her brother as a warrior. She lives solely to aid him and her people. And she is sacred, even as White Painted Woman. She is respected above all living women."[1]

● ● ●

A second band of *ricos* came in search of those who had died. The vultures and wolves had left little of the first party. They left little of the second. And all this was done without any Apaches being wounded.

Then Victorio gave orders to ride.

At our next camp the chief came to Grandmother and Nana. Lozen is as my right hand," he said. "Strong as a man, braver than most, and cunning in strategy, Lozen is a shield to her people."

Lozen also opposed the use of mescal and visiting in the villages, I learned from Grandmother. The people knew her wisdom and her ability as a warrior, but most of all they respected her Power. In some ways she was as formidable as her brother. Not only her prowess as a fighter, but her skill in dressing wounds, and her Power caused her to be revered. Many times I have seen her stand and determine the location of the enemy. With outstretched hands she would slowly turn as she sang a prayer:

> Upon this earth
> On which we live
> Ussen has Power.
> This Power is mine
> For locating the Enemy.
> I search for that Enemy
> Which only Ussen the Great
> Can show to me.

Our chief continued, "I depend upon Lozen as I do Nana. She is skillful in dressing wounds; when I got a bullet through my shoulder she burned the thorns from a leaf of *nopal,* split it and bound the fleshy side to the wound. The next day I rode."

"I'm glad Lozen is with us now," said Nana. "We need her help in locating the enemy. Attack may come from any source, and we are far from the high mountains."

"I think constantly of my wife and my little son. I left them in a safe place, for there was no time nor opportunity to go back for them."

"Why not go look for them?" asked Nana.

"My duty is to my people," Victorio answered. "My family must share the dangers just as others do."

"My brother is a chief first, a father and husband second."

"*Enjuh!* That is my intention."

Grandfather Nana's Power was to locate and capture ammunition trains. The value of his Medicine can hardly be exaggerated, for while rifles can be used indefinitely, ammunition is soon exhausted, and the supply must be replenished frequently. Nana could obtain it when all others failed. He also had Power over rattlesnakes. It was believed that he could handle them without being harmed, but I never saw him touch one. Contrary to general opinion, Apaches fear snakes. That is one of the reasons for their avoidance of night fighting and traveling, for in the hot desert, rattlesnakes lie hidden during the day and seek their food at night.

Grandmother's great Power was that of healing wounds. Mother's was in avoiding them. In all the skirmishes in which she fought beside my father, and later with Kaytennae, she never got a scratch. These great gifts had been given the women after they had been tested on the Sacred Mountain.

Though Power was bestowed for the benefit of the tribe, there were those who used theirs for evil; and these we regarded as witches. They were feared and shunned by all, and if found guilty of causing tragedy or sorrow, were banished.

It was to the Sacred Mountain that the young men went before beginning their apprenticeship as warriors. There they were sent to fast and pray, to be tested, and to receive some omen that would be of help to them before beginning to serve on the four raids required of the aspiring warrior. While it is true that all mountains were places of refuge, the Sacred Mountain was held in such great awe that people approached it in fear; for it was there that the Mountain Spirits dwelt, they who are the link between Ussen and Earth people.

Grandmother headed for the Mountain and pushed steadily forward, stopping only briefly at infrequent intervals. Improvident ones had failed to fill their jugs and had to be supplied with water. Weary ones begged for rest, timid ones urged another destination, but she ignored their murmurings. During that long trip I think I slept much of the time, snuggled against Grandmother's back, just as other children of the band riding behind their elders. Even the adults inured to long hours in the saddle, napped at times.

It was a weary and thirsty band that dismounted at the spring near the foot of the Mountain. Apaches can go long without food, but no creatures can go without water. Grandmother sent two young boys to reconnoiter before going near the spring. Then she permitted a few at a time to dismount and drink. She selected a camping place some distance from the water, and not visible from it. At its back was a cliff, at its front a mesquite thicket. Through it ran an arroyo deep enough to conceal fires and afford exits in case of attack. Only at midday did she permit fires to be lighted, and then only of very dry wood. Unlike White Eyes we never camped at the water's edge, and we never built big fires to frighten the game or betray our presence to the enemy. Ussen had given water not only to man but to all creatures. Except in extremity we did not kill animals at the drinking pool. We carried our water to a camp where there was grass, wood, and concealment.

Grandmother kept two young boys on the cliff as lookouts. They rubbed clay into their breech clouts, tied bunches of grass or feathers on their heads, and took their places on the ledges above us. Their bodies blended so nicely with the rock that unless one moved it was almost impossible to locate him. Each understood the importance of his vigilance, and was proud of his trust. I longed for the day when I could share such responsibility.

The women set about cutting brush and building arbors. Each of these faced the rising sun, as do all Apache dwellings. Our tepees, before they were destroyed by the cavalry, had done so. I could not remember having slept in a tepee covered with skins, though all our people had made them so before the Blue Coats came. Since then we had lacked enough hides even for clothing. To make breech clouts and shirts our people had traded for muslin with the store at Monticello. Muslin was used also — that and calico — for the women's dresses. But we had not learned to use any foot covering other than moccasins, and these had to be renewed or mended often.

The tanning of a hide is a slow and difficult process. Much buckskin is required for one pair of moccasins. The footgear was long and could be drawn up for warmth; or it could be folded below the knee for protection against thorns and rock. In those folds we carried our valuable possessions, valuable primarily in the sense of usefulness. Sometimes these included extra cowhide soles, for soles wore out quickly and had to be replaced. We carried the endthorns of a mescal plant with fiber attached for sewing the soles to the uppers. The soles were tanned with the hair left on, and they projected beyond the toes and terminated in a circular flap with a metal button sewed to the center. This piece turned back over the toes for additional protection. Because we frequently had to abandon our horses to scale cliffs, the moccasin was our most important article of dress.

Buckskin shirts, as well as the beaded robes of the women, were used for ceremonial attire. The calico shirt with a muslin breech clout supported by a belt, a headband to keep the long hair from obscuring the vision, moccasins, and one or more cartridge belts constituted the dress of the warrior. The Warm Springs Apaches, as a distinguishing mark wore a band of buckskin over the right shoulder. This was tied to the belt under the left arm, and was colored yellow by the sacred pollen of the *tule* [cattail] called *hoddentin*. This was a symbol of fertility. The blanket was not primarily an article of clothing, although we did, of course, use it for that purpose.

Women wore two-piece dresses made of calico. They made them with skirts long and full, such as the officers' wives wore. The blouse was also long and worn on the outside of the belt that supported the skirt. A knife was an essential part of each one's equipment and there were many women, such as Mother and Lozen, who had ammunition belts and rifles.

When not on guard duty the boys hunted with bow and arrows, or with slings. The latter was a formidable weapon and used extensively. So was the lance, though little mention is made of either, in books concerning the Apache. All were noiseless, and effective in killing game. Cattle could be killed with lances but that was strictly forbidden because the average Apache cowboy was regarded as much more daring and a better shot than the cavalryman.

Victorio had various means of securing arms and ammunition. The trader at Monticello could not supply all he needed, but there were sources in Mexico, and in other villages along the Río Grande, from which he could obtain them in return for protecting the inhabitants. And there were always the raids. Not within my memory were our primitive weapons of much use in fighting, but they served for training the boys in the art. And with us, fighting was of necessity an art.

While the cavalry was supplied with all its needs, we had to live off the land. Though meat was our favorite food, we also depended much upon mescal. This plant — maguey — is at its best when its blossom stalk bursts through the earth, but it is edible at any time. The women prepared it by cutting away the long, thorny leaves at the base, and leaving a large mass just above the ground. In Mexico the maguey stalks grow to the height and diameter of a telephone pole, but are smaller in our country. We had been accustomed to harvesting and preparing great quantities in the past, but when pursued by the enemy had to secure it as we could.

When a number of the maguey heads are collected, fires are built in pits and the wood burned to coals. Vegetation is thrown on the coals and the heads placed on top of the pile. More vegetation is added and the contents of the pit covered with earth and tamped. For testing the readiness of the mescal, long leaves of the plant are placed standing up in the pit with the fleshy end down, and occasionally withdrawn to check the progress of the cooking. Three or four days are required to cook many large heads, and during that time the pit must be watched to prevent the escape of heat and steam. When uncovered, the outer hull of leaves is discarded, leaving a mass of candied pulp containing fine fibers resembling shredded wheat. This mass is sliced and dried. It will keep indefinitely, and to our taste, is delicious. With a handful of mescal, and pounded, dried venison a man can run all day.

We used bags of cowhide for storing both meat and mescal. Pack animals carried these foods, and both families and individuals drew from the community supply as they needed rations.

Seed of various wild grasses was gathered by holding a basket under the heads and striking the grass sharply, but we did not depend much upon the seed for bread. We preferred acorn meal, and meal made from the mesquite bean. We gathered and dried berries in season. We also harvested the fruit of the *nopal* [prickly pear] and the saguaro cactus, both of which we liked very much. The latter grows in Arizona, but we were nomadic and when it was ripe, we went to it. Both dried fruits resemble figs. The only other sweet we had was wild honey, which we obtained by shooting arrows at the masses hanging from cliffs, and catching it on skins. We stored it in leather bags, and valued it highly.

Before being robbed of our lands by the White Eyes, my people went south for the winter, sometimes as far as the land of palms and oranges in Mexico. We harvested food as we went, and we stored surpluses in caches, preferably in caves near a water supply. We also left cooking utensils because pottery breaks easily.

And we stored blankets, bales of calico, and other commodities taken from smugglers who were constantly going back and forth in caravans. If our people were forced to flee they used these reserves.

One morning I was awakened by the sound of Grandfather's voice. He sat in the opening of our brush arbor, facing the rising sun, and singing The Morning Song. This is a hymn to Ussen thanking Him for one of the greatest of his gifts — the love between man and woman, which is to Apaches, a sacred thing. Never do they make obscene jokes about sex, and the fact that White Eyes consider conception and birth a matter of levity is something they cannot understand. It is, to them, on a level with taking the name of God in vain. I am very proud of the fact that in our language there is no profanity. For the privilege in sharing in the creation of new life we give thanks to the Creator of Life.

Grandfather brought my uncles, Blanco and Suldeen, with him. He brought also my paternal grandfather, Sánchez. Among the young warriors of his band was Kaytennae, already established as a potential leader.[2] Although Kaytennae was not descended from chiefs, leadership was not barred to him, for the position is elective. Said to be arrogant, Kaytennae was always modest and deferential to Nana. When the boys lined up to take the horses of the warriors, Kaytennae served Grandfather as he had before making the four raids required for qualifying him as a warrior. I had realized that Grandfather was pleased by Kaytennae's attitude, and longed for the time when I could act as his servant. I was constantly reminded that in order to lead well one must first serve well.

Kaytennae was equally courteous to Sánchez. It had never occurred to me to fear Nana, but I stood in awe of my other grandfather. Without knowing just why, I felt that Sánchez differed from the others of our band. Later I realized that his attitude was tinged by his years of living as a slave in Mexico. Nana told of his having been captured in Chihuahua when he attempted to rescue my father who was a child at the time. The Mexicans had captured several women and children; and they took Sánchez, also. Why they spared his life, in violation of their customary procedures, I never knew. He became a very efficient *vaquero,* knew all the trails, and protected the herd of his captor from raids. He became proficient in the language and skills of the people of Chihuahua. Time after time he could have escaped had he been willing to leave his small son, but that he would not do. Eventually they got away together and rejoined their people.

When the warriors met at Nana's fire for a council he motioned Sánchez to the place of honor. At his other side sat Blanco, because he was the Medicine Man. Suldeen and Kaytennae ranked next, and the others completed the semicircle. Grandmother served *tiswin* [fermented liquor made from sprouted corn] and food before the deliberations began. Then she seated herself behind Nana and drew me to her. When the men had eaten I saw her toe lightly touch Nana. He turned with a smile and asked Kaytennae to invite Lozen to the council.

Much has been written of the low regard in which Indian women were held. Among my people that was not true. Instead, they were respected, protected, and cherished. I knew of no other woman bidden to the council, but that was because no other had the skill as a warrior that Lozen did. She could ride, shoot, and fight like a man; and I think she had more ability in planning military strategy than did Victorio. At the time I speak of, she had not married, she went on the warpath with the men, which no woman other than the wives of warriors was permitted to do; and she was held in the greatest respect by them, much as though she were a holy person.[3]

But Lozen did not let the esteem in which she was held prevent her doing the tasks that of necessity fell to the women. Women did much hard work, but how else could have the tribe existed? Women prepared food, tanned hides, made clothing and built shelters. Has it not always been so among primitive peoples?

The men sat in silence until Lozen approached. She circled the group and took her place beside Grandmother. Nana began: "All know the situation. Victorio has refused to return to San Carlos as ordered by Washington. We went once to that place on the Gila where our people died like flies. Our chief prefers death in battle to bondage and starvation. When given his choice Loco agreed to go back to San Carlos. That was his privilege. It was also my privilege. But I leave the decision to you, my brothers, for no Apache is forced to fight. We are a free people. You all know that refusal to return to San Carlos means fighting — fighting to the death.

"If we refuse there is an alternative. The cavalry has orders to shoot on sight any Apache — man, woman, or child — seen off the reservation. We no longer have a reservation. But if our brothers, the Mescaleros, will admit us, we may have refuge with them. Does anyone know of another possibility?"

There was prolonged silence, finally broken by Sánchez:

"There is always Mexico. Sonora is a much better place than Chihuahua. Juh, chief of the Nednhi, is my friend. His stronghold is in the Blue Mountains which divide the two states. He has many good hideouts in that lofty range. Many of you have visited Juh and know that I speak the truth. You know that he controls the divide and that without his consent nobody crosses the Sierra Madre. From the east people go as far as Las Carretas, so called because carts must stop there. Horses can make that trail but no Mexican — not even the cavalry — travels it. They fear Juh, and they detour to the north. Neither do people from Sonora invade Juh's domain.

"Juh's favorite retreat is an immense flat-topped mountain upon which there is a forest, streams, grass, and abundance of game. To the top there is one trail and only one. It is a zigzag path, leading to the crest. Along it huge stones are poised so that even a boy could send them crashing down upon the trail. They would sweep before them everything — invaders, stones, trees, earth. Mexican troops tried it once. There are still bits of metal and bones at the foot."

"My brother speaks wisely," said Nana. "That refuge is always open to us. I have been there and Juh has said it to me. It is for our immediate need that we consider Mescalero — not for a permanent home, but for a temporary retreat. There are many of our people in hiding in the Black Range. They are without mounts, ammunition, or blankets. If we go at once to Mexico we must leave them. Should we do that?"

"There will be time enough when we have looked after their needs," said Sánchez.

Nana spoke: "There is a possibility that those at Mescalero may not admit us. In order to go to their reservation we must consult the head men: Natzili, the head Mescalero chief, named for the buffalo; Magoosh, Lipan chief from across the Pecos, and San Juan, if he is still living. If they consent to our coming, there is still the agent. I doubt that he will refuse, for the more Apaches he has enrolled on the reservation, the greater the opportunity of robbing them of the supplies furnished by the government. Then there is still Washington. From that place comes only evil, and we have had enough of that. Still, we must make the attempt. If you are agreed, whom shall we send to negotiate with the ones in control?"

He asked each in turn and the choice was unanimous — Nana. He turned his head. "And you, my niece?"

Lozen replied, "You are our chief. It is fitting that you intercede for us."

"Then it is decided. I may fail you — I can but do my best."

He turned to Kaytennae. "Be prepared to leave with me in the morning. Tonight I go to the mountain to pray."

He limped up the hill and I saw his tall, thin figure silhouetted against the moon. Then the darkness swallowed him and I knew he had circled the huge rock on the ledge. I knew, too, that he was standing with face and arms raised toward Ussen in supplication. The Apache did not grovel before the Creator of Life.

The group waited reverently for a few minutes; then Sánchez said, "I think our chief will succeed in his mission. I wish that Loco felt as he does. If he and his band spend a summer in that place of evils, there will be few left.

"And now, let us get some rest."

"*Enjuh!*" said the others.

And we went to our shelters.

Paul Blazer Photo

The Mescalero Apache Agency on the Tularosa, 1875

The Mescalero Reservation

In December, 1878, Nana took his Warm Springs band to the headquarters of the Mescalero Apache Reservation at Blazer's Mill on the Tularosa. He so distrusted White Eyes, and Indian agents especially, that he sent his young men and most of the horses over the saddle to the Rinconada from the west side. Then, with many of his people walking, he went through the little village of Tularosa and up the stream of that name to the mill.

There, as he had promised, Agent Godfroy enrolled sixty-three Warm Springs Apaches and arranged that rations be issued to them. He reported to the Commissioner of Indian Affairs that we had arrived emaciated from hunger and almost destitute of clothing, but that he found us surprisingly intelligent. He had talked with Nana and Sánchez through José Carillo, the interpreter, and may have had this information from him. Although both of my grandfathers have been accused of many things not greatly to their credit, lack of intelligence seems not to have been one of the criticisms. Mr. Godfroy may have judged the others by them.[1]

Nana either had anticipated or been told that his band would be located in the Rinconada. That canyon was remote, not so much in distance as in accessibility. There are many people living near the reservation today who sometimes have difficulty in finding that

[25]

hidden canyon. The road is still little more than a trail and is impassable much of the time. Before leaving, each man was registered, with the names of the women and children accompanying him.[2] Not long ago I read copies of the letters written to the Commissioner concerning our entry. These letters were written in ink, and were faded, but legible.

Ration cards were issued to the heads of each family and lists kept in the office. We camped about the mill until Saturday — Issue Day, when we took our places at the end of the long line of Mescaleros, filed past the window, and were given meat, flour, sugar, and coffee. Then we left for the Rinconada where, unknown to the agent, men and horses awaited us. Nana had not been asked if others had accompanied him; and there was the advantage of the warriors' being able to leave the reservation without being missed. Grandfather was wise in the ways of the agents.

My people set about constructing brush arbors. They banked them with soil taken from the fire holes in the centers, and stretched a few hides over them. Arbors are comfortable in summer, but without covering afford little protection from cold. There was an abundance of wood, water, and deer. As we killed game we added hides to the shelters. There was not much wind — just a still, dry cold. We lay with our feet toward the fire, huddled close for warmth.

Each Saturday morning, with me behind her, Grandmother led a pack animal to the agency. Mr. Godfroy occupied a room in one of Dr. Blazer's houses and used a small building for distributing supplies. They "issued" also flour, sugar, meal, green coffee, and salt. The flour was very inferior, being mostly bran, but it was food; we received enough to last three or four days. Without venison we might have suffered, but there were many deer. We were fortunate in that we were free from attack, and that we had an opportunity to replenish our scanty supply of clothing. Moccasins were the first essential, and the women set about making them. Without them we were as a cowboy without boots.

The agent promised blankets but they did not come until spring, and they were cheap and shoddy.

At that time the cattle on the reservation were not the property of the Mescaleros, but of White Eye ranchers who paid no grazing fees.[3] Why, then, should not the Indians have been permitted to kill a beef to satisfy their hunger? No Indian ever killed except for necessity. The agent forbade their stealing. Stealing! We had been robbed of land, freedom, and lives! He who steals millions is a hero and almost sure to be elected to high political office, but he who steals a chicken to satisfy his hunger is sent to the penitentiary. There is another custom incomprehensible to the Apache: it is that by which a piece of paper can compel a man whose word is not good to adhere to his promises. Even more is he confused when words can be so twisted that even the paper is worthless. We have seen this happen in something called an Executive Order, made and signed by the President of the United States, only to be broken whenever it was found profitable to cancel the promise. Great and mysterious are the ways of civilization!

Is it strange that my people distrust promises? Is it strange that they fear for the effects of education upon their young men? Have they not seen their sons so corrupted by the evil ways of White Eyes that they betray their own people to curry favors with agents and politicians? Have they forgotten that the great chief is he who gives most to his people rather than he who steals most from them?

During that winter in the Rinconada people gathered their children about the fires at night and told them the history and legends of our people. They recited their achievements, their victories, and their injustices at the hands of the white people, both Spanish and Anglo. I never tired of these stories. I listened to them over and over, until, if Grandfather were interrupted, I could supply the next sentence. I memorized them as my grandchildren do nursery rhymes and fairy tales.

Neither Nana nor Grandmother failed to emphasize our dependence upon Ussen, nor our obligation to be grateful to Him. Neither failed to pray to Him each day. We had nothing comparable to a church, but our people prayed habitually. I cannot remember when I was first taught to do so, nor when Grandmother first told me the stories of White Painted Woman and her Son, Child of the Waters.

She never failed, either, to recite the injustices of the white men and the wrongs we had suffered at their hands.

"Why does Ussen permit this?"

"That we do not know, Torres. He made this land and gave it to our people. The Creator of Life does not defend it for us, though. He expects us to do that for ourselves. Child of the Waters taught us to let others alone unless we were attacked; but He wants us to defend ourselves if we are. He gave us the bow and arrow, the sling and the spear, for that purpose. Victorio and Nana obey Him in defending their people. That is why they refuse to go to San Carlos."

"Where is San Carlos?"

"Far to the setting sun, on the Río Gila. It is a place of death. Few people can endure a summer there. Before you were born I went to that terrible place. There was nothing but cactus, rattlesnakes, heat, rocks, and insects. No game; no edible plants. Many, many of our people died of starvation. Victorio saw that if we stayed none would live so he took us and left. Even Loco, the Crazy One, joined us in that flight."

"Why is he called Loco?"

"Because he trusts the White Eyes."[4]

"Why do they want to put us there again?"

"So that we may die. Their alibi is that they wish to civilize us. That means they want to make thieves and liars of us like themselves. It means that those of us who live will degenerate. We will become weak and useless from the illnesses and vices of the White Eyes. It means that some may even turn against their own people to curry favor with the agents. They will see their own go hungry and lift no hand to help them. It means they will live only for themselves, selling the food needed by their brothers, even as the agents do. Torres, never trust a White Eye."

"Torres!" I had become conscious of the fact that mine was not an Apache name, but, like that of Sánchez, it was Spanish. Not until a boy insulted me did I go to Grandmother for an explanation.

"It is true that your name is Spanish, but you have no drop of white blood. Your grandfather lived long among the Mexicans, but you need not be ashamed, for you are of pure Apache blood. When you are older you will have an Indian name, but not until you have deserved it."

"How can I earn another name?"

"First, by obedience. An Apache obeys or dies. Not only his life but that of the tribe may depend upon his obedience and his truthfulness. In all your life nobody has ever struck you. Nobody will, unless you fail in the things that mean safety to the group. Few

Apaches ever strike a child, but for disobedience and lying they must, in order to protect the lives of all."

Vaguely I comprehended these things.

"Above all, you must be truthful. If you are you will be respected; and without respect no human relationship is of any value. No liar is permitted to give evidence in a trial, although he may have witnessed what occurred. No liar is ever permitted to carry messages for fear that he may endanger the whole tribe by not giving his message truthfully. The liar is despised by all.

"And you must be useful and observant. You see how the older boys compete for the honor of serving the warriors. They care for the horses, run the errands, cook the food, and try to anticipate and supply the needs of him whom they serve. They listen respectfully and ask no questions unless they are necessary for obeying commands. They eat poor food, fast for long intervals, are faithful in every way, and above all, do not discuss things they may overhear."

"When may I begin this training?"

"You have already begun it. I've taught you these things since I took you and released your mother to go on the warpath with your father. Continue to practice these things faithfully if you wish to become a warrior. Just this morning you showed plainly that you did not want to break the ice in the little stream and bathe with the older boys."

I was ashamed. I had shrunk from that ordeal, although I had finally endured it. I kept thinking how good it had been to slip into the lukewarm water of our Ojo Caliente, the spring near which I was born. Except for the times when it was reserved for the women, the boys spent much of their time in it; when women were using it no man nor boy approached it on penalty of death. Guards were stationed out of sight of the pool and the rule rigidly enforced.

The Ojo Caliente seeps from the foot of a little hill not far from Tall Mountain [San Mateo Peak], on the west side of the range. The natural basin from which we got our drinking water was perhaps ten feet in diameter. From it the water flowed into a much larger one in which we bathed. It overflowed to form the Cañada Alamosa. It has cut a channel through the mountains between precipitous bluffs far enough apart to permit the passage of a wagon. Ordinarily it is shallow enough to be waded. Through this gap the people of Monticello sometimes drove *carretas*. And once I drove up that stream and through that opening in a wagon.

The Warm Springs Apaches loved that spot, not only for its beneficient water but because it was a place of natural defense. If enemies approached from the west we had but to move through the gap and take refuge among the boulders. Those who attempted to follow us could easily be killed by rocks rolled from the top; and a similar protection was available from the east. For this reason it had been a favorite campsite for Juan José, Mangas Coloradas, Cuchillo Negro, and Victorio.

Not long ago I visited that spring. I stopped at Monticello and was kindly received by some of the very old residents of that little village. I had met these people when I went as a member of a committee from Fort Sill to select a home for my people about to be released from bondage. With Eugene Chihuahua and several others we went by train to Engle, and made the rest of the trip by wagon. That was in 1912. And in 1959, I found two old men[5] who remembered me, as well as Victorio and Nana. They advised me not to attempt to drive up the bed of the Alamosa, as I'd done in the wagon, but to take a circuitous route over the range to the spring. After crossing the divide and turning north we found only one ranch house on the twenty-five mile trip to Ojo Caliente.

Crumbling ruins south of the stream are all that remain of the adobe building which served both as fort and as headquarters for the Warm Springs Apaches. I passed only one car along that lonely highway. It is as calm and peaceful as I remember it; and despite the years of drought, the water supply was little diminished, although the spring at Fort Cummings was dry. I still regret that the decision of the majority of the committee resulted in the rejection of that place as a home for the few Warm Springs Apaches left alive at that time.

●　　●　　●

"Grandmother, who took our reservation?"

"White Eyes. Not from Mexico but Washington. Nothing good has ever come from that place."

That is what she told me when I was a small child.

I was asleep in my blankets when two young men came to Grandmother's camp in the Rinconada to deliver a message from

Victorio. She prepared food and water for them and they wrapped themselves in our blankets. I went for Nana. He would not permit them to deliver their message until they had rested enough to breathe easily. Then he cautioned them to take only sips of water and a few bites of food. Not until they had reported to him did he permit them to take a deep drink of water.[6]

Loco had started with his band to San Carlos and camped near Fort Cummings at the east end of Cook's Peak at the foot of Standing Mountain [Cook's Peak]. There his party was attacked by cavalry. Several were killed before he convinced the scouts that he was going voluntarily to San Carlos. The soldiers proceeded to escort his band toward the Gila. Victorio was informed by messenger of this and started to the rescue. A deep snow in the mountains forced the cavalry, encumbered with wagons, to run north to Fort Apache.

Grandfather mused. "Bad. But not so bad as San Carlos. Winters at the fort are cold, but there is abundance of wood at Turkey Creek. Soldiers are far more generous with rations than are civilian agents. There is much game near the fort. And there are our brothers, the Chiricahuas, and some Tontos. But there are also some of our enemies there."

One of the runners replied, "Victorio said the same. Loco and the women and children will not fare badly there. The trouble is that they may be moved to the Gila. The men didn't go in, anyway, except for a few of the older ones. Victorio says that so long as Loco remains at Fort Apache it may be best to leave him there; but if he is forced to San Carlos something must be done. Right now the Chief has not enough ammunition for an attempt to release them. Anyway they will be fed and provided with blankets for the winter. Meanwhile Victorio will lay in a supply of ammunition and other necessities; he will see that all the caches are stocked so that if Loco's band flees to Mexico they need not carry much with them."

"I will send the men to Victorio," Nana promised. "The Mescaleros know they are here, but the agent does not. They will not be missed when they leave."[7]

Again the messengers came with word that Victorio had captured an ammunition train. With thirty-five of his own men and several of Cochise's Chiricahua he went into Mexico and secured food, mules, and blankets. He was equipped to rescue his people before summer. They had been taken, as he foresaw, to Camp Goodwin, the post abandoned by the cavalry because of the "shaking sickness" that causes people alternately to freeze and burn. That sickness was caused by the insects with the long beaks.[8] They cause death. They almost devoured the babies taken there when Victorio went. It is because of the sickness that we must be put there — they wanted us to die.

"It is cruel to kill prisoners so," said Nicholas, a Chiricahua runner. "White Eyes accuse us of cruelty, but never have we done anything so bad. Blanco says that Child of the Waters forbade our killing prisoners who lay down their arms and quit fighting. He did not command us to endure anything like this."

Nana listened grimly.

"Has Victorio secured any promises as to our being given possession of the Ojo Caliente Reservation yet?"

"No. He bade us tell you that he has again communicated with the cavalry. He has agreed that if he may take his people to their home he will guarantee the peace, grant protection to those crossing his land, and keep his people within the bounds designated by the government. He has little hope that they will grant this, for miners are flocking in to despoil our mountains."

Nana nodded.

"The White Eyes are superstitious about gold. Their lust for it is insatiable. They lie, steal, kill, die, for it. If forced to choose between it and things many times exceeding it in value they unhesitatingly choose gold. Little do they care that they incur the wrath of the Mountain Gods."[9]

"Tell my Chief," Nana instructed, "that I have heard his orders and that I obey."

"Will the Mescaleros join you?"

"Their chief, Roman Chiquito, has advised his band not to do so. However, there are two other bands. Some of them may. For the present we are safe here. We have food, not enough, but some. We cannot afford to jeopardize our safety, such as it is, until Victorio orders us to join him."

At the fire that night Nana talked of Juh's stronghold in the Sierra Madre, picturing the peace and security there. He spoke of how we might live indefinitely even if the trail were destroyed and we were cut off from all the rest of the world. We would be as those who are gone to the Happy Place of the Dead — provided with all necessities, protected from all enemies.

"Could no one find us there?"

"Only the scouts, the accursed scouts.[10] When they first began working with the cavalry it was to run down our enemies. Now they are used against their own people, and for what? Only the silver — the eight pieces of silver they get every moon. They might guide the cavalry to the foot of that trail, but they could never climb it. They would be buried under a landslide if they attempted it."

"We would have everything on that mesa but ammunition," said Suldeen.

"We could live there without it. We lived well without it once. With no enemies we would not need it. We never went hungry in the old days before the White Eyes came. Up until that time we had never known hunger nor attack — to any great extent. Since their coming we have known little else."

"True."

Then Blanco spoke, "We have pledged our word to the Mescaleros that we will do nothing while on their reservation to bring trouble to them. They have forbidden the men of their bands to join us. For that we cannot be critical, for they have been driven from their homes, even as we, and know what it means to be hunted down like animals. If we could return to Ojo Caliente we would feel as they do. We are here on condition of causing them no trouble. We have given our word. We must keep that word."

"If we leave, we shall no longer be on their reservation," said Nana, quietly. "Instead we shall be in Mexico and we shall have kept our pledge to them. So long as we are here that promise will be scrupulously kept. We will ask no Mescalero to join us. We will endure without protest anything the agent does. We will show the Mescaleros and the White Eyes, too, that when an Apache chief pledges his word he makes it good. And that is more than their Great *Nantan,* the President, can say."

"*Enjuh!*" said Blanco.

"*Enjuh!*" said the rest.

Carrizo Gallarito, a Mescalero Apache called
Crook Neck by his people, was a good friend
to the Warm Springs Apache.

The Ceremonials

During that cold winter Nana frequently came and went from the reservation. Shortly after we arrived he rode in with quantities of food and blankets which he divided with the Mecaleros. The supplies, he said, were rightfully ours to share. They had been appropriated by Mr. Godfroy and sold to a wholesaler in Las Cruces. The agent had sent them by wagons to the Río Grande with Mescaleros driving.

Among the Mescaleros was my good friend, Carrizo Gallarito, called Crook Neck by his people. He was the youngest of those ordered to take the food for disposal, all of whom knew that it had been sent for the use of the Indians. Not one dared protest or refuse to do anything ordered by the agent. They delivered the supplies to the wholesaler's warehouse and returned, but each had a plausible excuse for not making a second trip, and others were sent with the next cargo. How many trips were made I do not know, but on one of them, not far from La Luz, Grandfather surprised and relieved them of the supplies they hauled without firing a shot. The hauling ceased.*

---

*In Mr. Godfroy's letters to the Commissioner I found no reference to this, but aged people on the reservation when Kaywaykla was telling his story still remembered it. Crook Neck was one of them, when he was almost 100 years old.

For the annual ceremony of the Apache maidens, Dorothy
Kaywaykla, the narrator's granddaughter, wears the traditional
robe and moccasins of buckskin, trimmed with beads and cone-
shaped tin jingles.

Reports of Indian atrocities did not originate with Anglo or Spanish people near Mescalero, for with them the Indians were on good terms. My people were illiterate and had no way of defending themselves against false accusations. They still have no means of doing so — not if they live on reservations. And, of course, they had no way of knowing what was reported to Washington.

Records show that Dr. Blazer bought a sawmill on the reservation in 1868 and a year or so later began operating it. The Apaches did not molest him.[1] The Mahill family* had lived in the Sacramentos a short time and had no trouble. Along the Ruidoso, Bonito, and Hondo Rivers there were settlers who lived at peace with the Indians. The agents themselves had no cause to complain, for I never heard of one's being molested. Mr. Godfroy wrote repeatedly to the Commissioner of Indian Affairs requesting that he be supplied with rifles and ammunition.[2] He stated that he had none except for hunting. He asked for eight — no more, and that possibly because of Nana's taking the food. He had a telegraph line to Fort Stanton, usually in condition for use. Occasionally the line was cut for the copper wire which made bright bracelets — not for the purpose of stopping communication. The Apaches needed jewelry for the ceremonies of the young maidens.

This presentation of the young women eligible for marriage is one of the oldest, and most sacred of our rites. That year the Mescaleros had several girls to present; my cousin, Siki, was the only one from among us. For weeks Grandmother had worked on her robe. It consisted of long beaded buckskin moccasins, an upper garment, and a two-piece skirt, trimmed in long fringe cut from the skin, with beads and hundreds of tiny cone-shaped tin jingles. Each jingle had a string of skin drawn through it and knotted to prevent its loss, leaving an inch-long strip to sew to the skirt. I think I chewed sinew all that winter to soften it for use in sewing.

The upper garment was made of a long piece of the leather with a slit cut crosswise for the head, and the ends hanging in front and back. Fringe fifteen inches long covered the arms and hung in graceful rows along both sides of the garment. Siki wore two eagle plumes floating from her long hair, and many silver and turquoise

*The village named for this family is called Mayhill because of an error in spelling that was made when the post office was established, according to a descendent, Frank Mahill.

ornaments which I did not remember having seen. They had been carried in the folds of Grandmother's moccasins.

The evening before the beginning of the four-day ceremony Nana told the story of its origin. Out of respect to the Mescaleros Grandfather gave their version of it which differs only slightly from ours. This is how it is told:

In the Guadalupes there is a mountain with a rock formation resembling a huge face [Guadalupe Point]. It keeps perpetual watch for enemies from the east. In our language it is called Say-a-chee. It is a Sacred Mountain, even as the one in the San Andres. From a cave beneath that great face come sounds of singing and dancing such as occur in our sacred rites. Many Apaches had heard those sounds and were curious about them, but nobody had had the courage to enter that place.

Long ago some Warm Springs had visited their brothers and were told of the cave. Among them was a wise and good woman, a medicine woman — E son kñh sen de hē. She decided to visit the cave. Her friends tried to dissuade her but could not. They accompanied her to the foot of the cliff where she told them to wait and pray for her return. They obeyed, for her Medicine was good and her Power great.

While she was gone they heard the songs and the drums, and experienced queer sensations just as the Mescaleros had described them. This was understandable, for the sounds were not made by Earth People.

She was gone so long that they thought her dead. They were happy when they heard her call to them; then she appeared with a lamb in her arms. They waited respectfully for her to speak about her experience in the cave, but were too polite to question her. Apaches tell what they wish — nothing more. Her friends noticed that after this visit the Medicine Woman's cures were many, and her good deeds multiplied.

The Warm Springs people returned to their camp near Mount Meteor, in their own country. The Medicine Woman called them together and told them what Ussen had commanded: that she climb that wall and pray to the Creator of Life.

"But that is impossible, my sister. No man has ever scaled that precipice."

"Ussen has spoken. I obey."

"Then let one man, or more, go with you."

"Only Ussen can help me. Stay at the foot and pray for me."

They watched her climb the steep slope to the foot of the cliff. There she lifted her arms and eyes, and she prayed. She began climbing, clinging to the wall, and finding first one foothold, then another. Far above her an opening appeared in the solid rock. Leading toward it she found steps, toeholds not there before. Sometimes it looked to those below that she could go no further, but always when her foot felt for a niche it found one.

She reached the opening to the cave which was guarded by a huge bear on either side. Beyond the bears she saw a pair of mountain lions, then two huge snakes, and beyond them two more that we do not name. To enter she must pass between the rows of beasts. She was frightened, but she walked calmly with bowed head. The door closed behind her, but there was light in the cave. She could see dimly the rows of Mountain Spirits between whom she must walk.

"What does our daughter seek?" they asked.

"That which will benefit my people."

"We have the Power; each of us has a different Power. We can bestow upon you only one. Speak."

"What Power have you?"

"That of healing smallpox. Others have other Powers."

"All are good; but I seek that which heals sickness of the Spirit."

Not until she reached the last aged woman did she find what she sought.

"My daughter, do you realize what you ask?"

"Perhaps not, Mother; but in your infinite wisdom you know what will bring the greatest good to my people."

"I do. If you had not been virtuous you would never have returned from the cave in the Guadalupes. If you had not been brave you would never have entered this place. What you ask I shall give. It is this: at times your people may have direct communication with the Mountain Spirits."

"How can that be? We are Earth People."

"You are of Earth, but you have reached this place where no other before you has been deemed worthy to come. We will come to you. Listen, remember, and obey: When your young girls have attained womanhood you are to make a feast for the worthy — the chaste. You will observe the rite of which I tell you. It is for the maidens, their sponsors, and the medicine men. It is to commemorate the sanctity of the gift of producing new life. The medicine men are to sing many prayers, a hundred seventy-four, or more, during the four days of the ceremonial. You are to teach them these songs. While they sing the maidens are to dance, and the fourth night the singing is to continue until dawn.

"During this rite the men will retire to a secret place and dress for their dance. There are to be four groups of four men each, for four is your sacred number. They will wear buckskin skirts, moccasins, and a mask surmounted by a high crown of sticks, painted with sacred symbols. No red is to be used.[3] Their bodies are to be blackened and symbols painted upon chest and back.

The men are to be accompanied by one or more clowns, with bodies painted white, and heads covered with masks. These will be boys learning the rites so that they may in time be admitted to the company of the dancers. They are to serve the men, to return to them any wand that may be dropped by the dancers, and to relieve the solemnity of the occasion.

"This dance is to be performed only after night has fallen. The participants are to be treated with the respect that would be shown if they were the Mountain Spirits they impersonate. No sign of recognition may be given them, not even by their mothers.

"Through the minds of the dancers, messages will be transmitted to the minds of the maidens who for the four days partake of the qualities of White Painted Woman. The maidens will tell the medicine men of the messages they receive, and these must be obeyed, for they are for the benefit of the entire tribe. All who attend the dances will receive good."

"All? The evil, too?"

"All. Even though an enemy be present he is to participate in the blessings."

Then she gave the woman songs and symbols, more information than any one mind could have retained without Divine aid, and the Medicine Woman returned to her people.

And again the cliff became unscalable.

•   •   •

Siki was prepared for the rite by rigid questioning from Grandmother as to her worthiness to participate — virginity being a first requisite. When Grandmother was satisfied, the young girl's hair was washed with fragrant suds made from the root of the yucca, and her body bathed with it. She was dressed in her beautiful costume and adorned with silver and turquoise. In a fold of her moccasin she carried some uncut turquoise.

I was awakened before dawn to see the erection of the ceremonial tepee. My uncle, Blanco, stood beside Gregorio, Medicine Man of the Mescaleros, to preside. About them stood the young men learning the songs and prayers of the rite. Twelve long poles were set in place and fragrant boughs fastened about the base and attached to poles leading from the entrance. In the center of the tepee the fire hole was dug, and behind it blankets spread for the maidens and their sponsors. At the left of the opening similar preparations were made for the medicine men, but the right side was left open for those who wished to enter and receive the blessings that Ussen enables the maidens to bestow during the four days. During the ceremonial they share the attributes of White Painted Woman, Mother of all Apaches, through her Son, Child of the Waters.

After skins were spread over the tepee, the chiefs joined the medicine men. A magnificent figure clad in white breech clout and moccasins, heavily beaded appeared. A scarlet blanket was thrown over his left arm; and a scarlet band held his long loose hair in place. Victorio! I had never seen my chief dressed otherwise than his men, and did not recognize him at first. I had heard Grandmother speak of that blanket — the gift of Manuelito, Chief of the Navajos. Victorio was not as tall as Naiche, but I think he was the most nearly perfect human being I have ever seen. No Greek statue had greater majesty of form and bearing.*

Behind him came Grandfather, similarly attired; then the others. I realized that my people were beautiful. I had never thought of them so before. Dimly I sensed pride in my race and heritage.

At the first glimmer above the eastern horizon Blanco lifted his face and arms in prayer. The group joined his song; and when it

*Kaywaykla presumably had seen Grecian sculptures on a visit to New York City and the museums there.

had ended, the maidens, with fire sticks, lighted the sacred blaze. Then each, attended by her sponsor, filed before the medicine men to receive her blessings, as the sacred pollen, symbol of fertility, was put upon her face. The maidens in turn blessed the men. The long line filed past to present themselves and their children for healing. Grandmother took my hand and joined the supplicants. We were the last.

The maidens lay prone upon blankets before the tepee while their sponsors kneaded the muscles of their backs in preparation for the four runs they were to make. One of the medicine men took the sacred basket and stood beside it, facing the girls. Four times they circled him and returned to their positions at the tepee.

Four days our people feasted and danced. Four evenings the four groups of four each performed the Dance of the Mountain Spirits.* Before dressing for the rite they retired to the mountainside and sent a scout to ascertain if preparations for their arrival had been completed. When the singers and drummers were ready, four men and a clown appeared from the east and circled the fire, leaping and stamping in time to the music, and brandishing the long wand they carried in each hand. From each of the four directions they approached the fire making ululating sounds as they advanced toward it. This was repeated by each group until all four had danced. When the men had completed the long, elaborate ritual, they disappeared in the forest to dress.

Medicine men, maidens, and sponsors retired to the tepee to begin their songs and dances. While the men sang, the maidens stood and performed simple gliding steps sidewise and back without lifting their feet. While the singing continued the maidens danced, but the men gave them frequent rest periods during which they were seated. For three nights this rite continued until midnight; upon the fourth it was not finished till dawn.

The medicine men had prepared one hundred seventy-four small sticks and placed them upright by the fire hole. As each song was completed a stick was removed. Upon the fourth night if the men finished the routine before dawn, they were to improvise more so that the sun might find them still singing. For my people this was not a difficult thing, for they are accustomed to doing it.

---

*Sometimes erroneously called the Devil Dance or Crown Dance.

The spectators were seated about the fire in a large circle, and after the Mountain Spirits left they began the social dances. They usually begin by joining hands, standing shoulder to shoulder, and shuffling about the fire, clockwise. The step is very simple and I caught it easily. Those who wish sit wrapped in blankets and watch, or join in the singing.

In the back-and-forth dance, women choose their partners and the men are obligated to pay them. Young girls sometimes receive valuable gifts, horses or blankets. Matrons are content with less, having been the recipients of presents before their marriages.

This is the first presentation rite that I remember, and it made a deep and lasting impression. I became aware of the majesty of a chief and the dignity and beauty of my people. I had seen them only in rags, hunted, oppressed, and unhappy. Even so they never lacked dignity, but I am sure it was increased by their participation in the traditional rites, and also by their clothing. I saw Grandfather in a new light. He had been a tall, thin, worn figure who limped slightly. Standing beside his chief he was scarcely less impressive than Victorio. I was proud of my grandfather and my uncle. I was beginning to understand what grandmother meant by the carriage and manner of a chief.

Siki, too, had taken on a new importance.

"Did Ussen speak to her?" I asked.

"Ussen spoke; but she can give the message only to the medicine men. During those four days your cousin was as White Painted Woman in her Power to do good for her people. Now she is just Siki, a girl eligible for marriage."

"And she will have a husband?"

"Yes; but not for at least two years. I shall not permit her to marry sooner."

The chief and the warriors departed, and with them my father, but this time Mother remained with us. I had seen little of her for she had accompanied my father to fight beside him. I still depended upon Grandmother for care and for stories. She took me with her to the agency as usual. When we went in for rations we found that there was a new man in charge, a man with long whiskers. I can not tell you the repulsion with which we regarded people with hair on their faces. To us it was repulsive, animal-like. He stood watching as we went past the window and received our rations. His long beard waved in the wind, and I wondered if it were true that White Eyes had no hair on their heads where it belongs. I had heard the warriors say they do not. This new agent wore a hat, and I could not see any hair except a sort of fringe on the back of his neck.

José Carrillo [the interpreter] came by as we were tying the food on the horse. Grandmother asked if Mr. Godfroy were in jail. José looked at her curiously, and then he smiled.

"Why would he be in jail?"

"For stealing our food," she replied, bravely.

"So it was Nana," he commented. "I thought so." Grandmother made no reply.

"Godfroy is not in jail," José said. "Who ever heard of an Indian agent's being punished for anything? No, he was permitted to resign."

History From Our Angle

I learned the history of my people about the fires at night. Word for word I could repeat many of the stories long before I understood the significance of them. They began with our legends of creation and our religion. They dealt with the wild, free life before the coming of the White Eyes. My people spent their summers in the mountains of New Mexico, carefree, untrammeled. They migrated to Mexico in the fall, living off the land as they went, killing game, harvesting fruit, and giving thanks to Ussen for the good things He had given. They knew the land of jungles and of tropical fruit. They knew the people whose land they crossed. They were on the very best of terms with Cochise and his band. They penetrated the fastnesses of Juh, Chief of the Nednhi, and were received as brothers. When they in turn came to us we gave freely of our best. So close were we with both that White Eyes have classified us as Chiricahua, which we were not. Only Cochise's and Chihuahua's bands were true Chiricahua.

There came a great war when white men fought white, and their troops were withdrawn from our territory. Mangas Coloradas and Cochise thought that at last the invaders were giving up the attempt at conquest, and they rejoiced. Their happiness was not to last long. The White Eyes returned in hordes to take our land from us. At first the lure was minerals in our mountains; later the land

[45]

itself was wanted for grazing. It was the prospectors and miners whom we considered most objectionable, for they grovelled in the earth and invoked the wrath of the Mountain Gods by seeking gold, the metal forbidden to man. It is a symbol of the Sun, of Ussen Himself, and sacred to Him. Apaches wear silver ornaments, but not gold. Many of my people know today where there are large deposits of it, but not one would touch it.

Even before the Civil War, long before, copper had been discovered and the Mexicans mined it in the land of Mangas Coloradas. They built a fort, houses, and corrals. They sent mule trains laden with ore to Durango to be smelted.[1] They sent others to Chihuahua for supplies.

They invited the chief and his people to a feast and promised gifts. The women and children assembled in an open place where corn and other things were piled for distribution. Few men responded to the invitation to take what they wished. Instead they kept to the edges, watching. A concealed howitzer was fired into the group of Apaches, killing and wounding many, and causing the rest to flee. Two wives of the chief were killed, but his infant son was rescued. Not until Mangas Coloradas was far from the scene of the massacre did he discover that the baby he carried with him was his son. I had this story from Mangus, his son, whom I knew well.[2]

The White Eyes had done this savage thing to procure the bounty offered by the governor of Chihuahua for Apache scalps. It is said that the Indians of the Great Plains practiced scalping, but it definitely was not an Apache custom. If it were resorted to by some, as is alleged, it was done for retaliation. But I doubt very much that many scalps were taken by Apaches. I have seen hundreds of people killed but not one scalped.[3] And I was with Victorio until his death, with Nana for years, and Geronimo several months.

Mangas Coloradas rallied his forces and waited. When a mule train of ore left the copper mine it did not return. The Mexicans waited long for it and for the supplies they needed. They posted extra guards, and they kept within their walls. When their food was exhausted they loaded what they could upon their horses and mules and abandoned the mine. Many set out for the border, but not one reached it. Not one.

After a few years White Eyes came. Mangas Coloradas had

no quarrel with them. He sincerely wanted peace. He trusted them to the extent of going alone to their camp. Both Victorio and Geronimo pleaded with him not to trust them. Even Loco opposed his going, but he went. The chief was an old man and one of great dignity. The White Eyes bound him to a tree and lashed him with ox goads until his back was striped with deep cuts. He crept away like a wounded animal to let his wounds heal. He went to his favorite camping site — near the Ojo Caliente, and there he stayed until the wounds were healed. Victorio knew; he knew, too, that the chief must not know that he did lest his heart break with shame. Never before had anyone struck him, and there is no humiliation worse than that of a whip.

After that came the war and the withdrawal of troops from our country. The truce did not last long. A new menace appeared, this time from the west. The California Column, under command of Colonel Carleton, left the Colorado River for the Río Grande. When a runner brought word to the chief he went to Cochise, the Chiricahua chief. He had previously submitted a plan for eliminating the soldiers, but Cochise had not accepted it, though he had married the daughter of the chief. Cochise listened courteously to his father-in-law, but showed no inclination to join him. At last the old chief stood, turned his back, and dropped his blanket.

Cochise summoned his warriors.

If the cavalry left Tucson for the Río Grande, as the Apaches anticipated, they would pass through a canyon in the land of Cochise, one in which there was a spring. It was the only water within many miles, and for that reason the road was traveled extensively. The chiefs prepared an ambush at Apache Pass. They would have had an easy victory had the White Eyes not produced a new and terrible weapon — cannon. Shells crashed into the hill sides upon which they lay concealed, dislodging stone and sending earth crashing down the slopes. The Apaches withdrew, carrying their wounded. The cavalry reached the spring. They reported that they had killed many Indians, but my people who were present say that not one of their warriors was killed.[4] Mangas Coloradas was wounded but his men removed him to a place of shelter.

A detachment of cavalry went northeast into our country. The main body proceeded to Mesilla, on the Río Bravo. When he recovered sufficiently to ride, Mangas Coloradas decided to go to the

White Eye camp and attempt to secure peace for his people. Despite the pleas of his sub-chiefs* he went, this time under promise of protection. As Victorio had anticipated, they killed the old chief and buried his body. Then they exhumed it, cut off his head, and boiled it in a great black pot.[5] This his scouts reported to Victorio.

The killing of an unarmed man who has gone to an enemy under truce was an incomprehensible act, but infinitely worse was the mutilation of his body. Most Apaches believe that the body will go through eternity in the condition in which it leaves the earth, and for that reason they abhor mutilation. Little did the White Eyes know how they would pay when they defiled the body of our great chief!

Victorio succeeded him though Cuchillo Negro exercised the leadership for a time. Both Nana and Loco led bands and at times joined Victorio. They joined him in cultivating peaceful relations with the people of Monticello and other Mexican villages, some of which had been in existence for two hundred years. Occasionally Mexicans came to our camp and our people went to their villages to trade.

Writers have extolled Carleton as a hero, but my people did not see him in that role. He was determined to exterminate them. He persuaded leaders in Washington that the Apaches should be confined in a camp at the Bosque Redondo on the Pecos. My people seldom went that far east, for there were no mountains. And to them mountains meant comparative safety. Carleton planned to put all Apaches there, but he reckoned without Victorio. Our chief agreed to meet him in council, but Carleton did not come; he sent others. Nana and Loco accompanied the chief to the meeting with Carleton's envoys. To them he made no promises, for he had no intention of taking his people to that place.

In 1863 about four hundred Mescaleros were taken there, and a year or two later eight thousand Navajos. They were enemies, but what difference did that make to Carleton? Or what cared he that the Navajos outnumbered the Apaches and that they stole the animals of the Apaches? Or that the place might have furnished sufficient food for four hundred but no more? Starving and destitute of clothing the Mescaleros endured the situation until the Navajos

---

*Although Kaywaykla used the term, Chihuahua and Daklugie insisted there had been no sub-chiefs.

contracted smallpox from the soldiers. They died by hundreds. Their bodies were thrown into the river from which the Mescaleros got their water. They knew nothing of germs, but much of the dangers of sickness. They took what they could carry and fled to their old campsite on the Bonito, above Fort Stanton.

In 1870 Washington promised Victorio that if his people would stay on a reservation they would be furnished with food, and would be given a thousand blankets. They were to have headquarters at Ojo Caliente; and Cochise, too, was to have a reservation about his stronghold. The acceptance of the terms meant the relinquishment of a vast territory which both chiefs knew they would eventually lose, but the certainty of a small portion of their land's being assured to them. Their people were decimated, war-worn, hungry, ragged, and discouraged. Many of their men opposed the decision, but the promise of food and blankets placated them to a certain extent.

Victorio was promised his reservation so long as the mountains should stand and the rivers exist. This promise was secured by a piece of paper called an Executive Order. The emissaries explained to the chief that it was signed by the President of the United States, was the equivalent of a treaty, and was the highest law of the land. As Victorio feared, the word of the white nantan was worthless — as worthless as the paper which he had accepted.

Then Vincent Colyer, Commissioner of Indian Affairs, came to Ojo Caliente where an adobe building had been erected to serve as headquarters of the tribe. He gave orders that Victorio was to take his people to the long narrow valley of the Tularosa River, high in the mountains to the west, and habitable only in summer. He explained that by another Executive Order our land had been returned to the public domain. Grimly our chief took his band to that wretched place. The promised supplies, so desperately needed in winter, did not reach them till spring, and were very inferior. Half-starved and half-frozen, people died during that terrible winter. Even the agent realized the enormity of the crime against them and protested it.

For a short time they were permitted to live again at Ojo Caliente. Gordo and his band joined them there. Geronimo came in from Mexico with horses, many horses. Victorio and about four hundred of the Warm Springs were camped a few miles from the fort. Many of the warriors were hunting in the mountains. Nobody was making any trouble. Victorio received word that Mr. John

Clum, agent at San Carlos, had given orders for him to come in and bring his people. He sent runners for the braves and took his band to the headquarters. There all of the leaders were placed under arrest.

Geronimo, Gordo, and Ponce, with five others, were chained and kept under guard in the corral. Victorio, Nana, and Loco were also under arrest but not confined. If the melodramatic scene described as Mr. Clum's "capture of Geronimo" occurred no Apache knew of it, and about five hundred witnessed the event.

The shackled prisoners were hauled to San Carlos; the rest walked.

They were forced to travel slowly, and upon their arrival learned that the eight men sent there by wagon were prisoners in the guardhouse. Victorio deeply and sincerely desired peace, and made no protest.

Just today I read a true account of the reasons for our having left our reservation.

Our people were put at old Camp Goodwin, which had been abandoned by the cavalry because of the many deaths from malaria. There they underwent the tortures of a summer where the temperatures sometimes reaches a hundred-forty degrees. There was no game, no food except the occasional meager and unfit stuff issued to them. The insects swarmed about them and almost devoured the babies.

Owen Wister has described that place as follows: "The Creator did not make San Carlos. It is older than He. When He got around to it after dressing up Paradise with fruit trees He just left it as He found it as a sample of the way they did jobs before He came along. He did not do any work around there at all. Take stones and ashes and thorns, with some scorpions and rattlesnakes thrown in, dump the outfit on stones, heat the stones red hot, set the United States Army after the Apaches, and you have San Carlos."

As agents went, John Clum was one of the best. The Apaches conceded that; but they knew also that he was responsible for the Chiricahua's reservation being taken from them, and that he caused the removal of Apaches from Cochise's reservation to San Carlos so that they would be under his jurisdiction. And they knew, too, that his motive for attempting to bring all Apaches under his rule was an increase in salary; they knew, too, that he did not get it.

They respected the arrogant young man in spite of that, for he was both courageous and honest. They believed him to be unique in that respect, having dealt with many of the breed. They liked his using Indian police and Indian judges. At that time both press and pulpit were debating the question of whether or not Indians possessed souls and it was commendable to have a man who realized that our standards differed from theirs and felt that a man should be judged by the mores of his people. Our standards were, at that, not so vastly different from those of the White Eyes except for the fact we set great store by promises and rigidly enforced chastity.

If Tom Jeffords, friend of Cochise and agent for the Chiricahua Reservation, could have replaced Mr. Clum, history might have been very different; but he, too, was honest and did not seem fit for the Indian Service.[6] Cochise had the promise of his head men to support Tahza for the leadership, and he had groomed the older son to replace him. When Cochise died the boy was too young to lead the Chiricahua, and Juh took the responsibility. I doubt that he was elected;* he was dominant, capable, and daring. The Chiricahua accepted his leadership until they were forced to go to San Carlos. Then Juh took many of the warriors and went to his old haunts in Sonora. Tahza and Naiche, the younger son of Cochise, went to San Carlos with their people. So did Jasper Kanseah, who was the nephew of Geronimo, and who went on the warpath with his uncle when he was about thirteen. He was my very good friend and I visited him often at Mescalero before he passed away last fall.

Before Mr. Clum left San Carlos he took about twenty young men to Philadelphia to the Exposition. When their people saw their young chief and his men depart they mourned for them as dead, for their experiences had caused them to feel that they were being taken away to be executed. The venture did not prove to be profitable and Mr. Clum took them to Washington. There Tahza sickened and was taken to the hospital where he died of pneumonia.

When it was reported that Mr. Clum had returned to San Carlos with all the dancers but the young chief, Tahza's brother Naiche went to the office to investigate. Naiche was not admitted. For three days he stood at the door and Mr. Clum refused to see him. That insolence was never forgotten. It increased the suspicion

---

*Daklugie said that the band that refused to go to San Carlos elected Juh as Chief.

that Tahza had been poisoned — that he had been taken away for that purpose. When Mr. Clum finally did explain the situation to Naiche, he did not believe the agent's story.

"I put him in a hospital where he had the best of doctors and the best of care. He died of pneumonia. I gave him a fine funeral and the great chiefs of the white people attended it to do him honor."

Naiche did not believe a word of it. Neither did the other Chiricahua. A fine funeral! Did that restore a beloved brother to Naiche? Did it bring back a young chief to his people?

That horrible summer! Victorio saw his people die. He saw babies almost devoured by insects. He saw people suffer from malaria, and that the medicine men could not save their lives. As long as he had hope of being returned to Ojo Caliente he encouraged his people to endurance, but when that failed he turned to Nana who had long urged him to take the people and flee. Even Loco acquiesced in the plan, and they made preparations for the flight. They had a few hidden rifles and a little ammunition. But they lacked horses. Knowing that they must depend upon speed rather than defense they took some from the cavalry and left the camp at sundown, by way of Ash Creek, with the intention of going to Mexico. When they discovered by the dust that they were being cut off from the south, they turned toward their old home. They covered their trail so well that their pursuers continued southward.

They kept to the ridges, using cover. When the aged were unable to keep the pace they left them in hidden places near water, with two young boys for protection. Encumbered as they were with women, children, and the aged they evaded the cavalry for weeks, picking up ranch horses as they went.

When they could find no game they killed cattle, and when without beef they ate horse meat. The cavalry reported that the band killed fifty-six people during that flight. After they had completely exhausted their supply of ammunition they encountered a group of ranchers near old Fort Wingate. Armed only with primitive weapons they killed twelve men and captured over a hundred horses. They maintained the unequal struggle until troops of cavalry overtook them and imprisoned them.

The Army fed them until November, 1877, and then returned them to Ojo Caliente. That winter they lived quietly in hiding, molesting nobody. Victorio still hoped for the restoration of his reservation. He went alone to a young officer whom he had learned to respect during the time he was at Fort Wingate. He knew the man to be sympathetic and hoped that he could help regain the land taken from the Apaches.

The officer spoke Spanish, and explained in that language that Victorio should take his people and return to San Carlos before orders were received to hunt them down.

"But we *are* in our own land, Capitán. This is the place that was promised to me and mine so long as the mountains stand and the rivers are here. Look out the door. Are not both still there?"

"They are, Victorio. Your claim is just, but I am a soldier and must obey orders just as your warriors do when you issue commands. I understand well why you are called the Conqueror, and I admire and respect you. But I am just a soldier. Orders are that every Apache, man, woman, or child, found off the reservation is to be shot without being given a chance to surrender."

"We are on our reservation."

"It has been taken from you."

"You are a good enemy," said Victorio. "It is good to know there is one honorable White Eye. You have been fair with me. I will be fair with you. I will not go to San Carlos. I will not take my people there. We prefer to die in our own land under the tall, cool pines. We will leave our bones with those of our people. It is better to die fighting than to starve — I have spoken."

"I have heard. There is one more thing I will tell you, even though it may cost me my commission. There is a reservation near the White Mountain across the Río Grande."

"I know."

"If you can get permission to take your band there, you may have safety and security there."

In the strange manner of the White Eyes they shook hands, and Victorio returned to his people. Nana immediately consented to go to the Mescalero Reservation, but Loco started voluntarily for San Carlos.

It was shortly after this that our camp was attacked.

Witchcraft

Nana and the warriors were mounting their horses to leave the reservation. I stood beside Grandmother, watching.

"Go to Nana and your father," she said.

Each took me in his arms as man does man. Grandfather led the way, but my father pulled his horse aside till all had passed. We watched the line wind up the path toward the saddle separating the Rinconada from the west slope of the mountain. My mother joined us and put her arms around me. My father turned and waved to us. We watched until he was gone from our sight.

"Why didn't you go with Father?" I asked.

She did not answer. I looked at her and saw that she was crying.

"We are never to see him again," she said.

"Why do you think that?"

"Ussen has spoken," she replied. And she went to the arbor.

Just how our people know these things I cannot explain, but I have seen proof of it many times.

After the men left I was very lonely. I was not old enough to be given a bow and arrows, not even to be trusted with a sling. I participated in games such as creep and freeze, taught us primarily for the purpose of enabling us to live. I had asked Grandfather when I might have a spear, but he had only smiled and shaken his head.

Sticks and stones were available, and I made use of them. One day I picked up a piece of well-blanched bone. Its rounded side just fitted my hand. I liked the big teeth on it. When we played at war it made a decided impression on the other boys. I kept it in my belt until Blanco spied it. He called me to him and examined it.

"It is an evil thing, Torres. Throw it into the fire."

It was my only possession and I did not obey until Grandmother nodded.

Blanco said, "I will sing four songs so that there may be no bad effects. That bone was the jaw of a bear, and it will bring harm to you. In the future you are never to eat the meat from the head of any animal. If you do so, great harm will result. See that you do not forget."

"Bear is very different from other animals. We do not eat its meat. We do not kill it except in self-defense. A bear is very much like a person. It can walk erect. We speak of its forelegs as arms, never as feet."

"Why, Grandmother?"

"Some of us believe that when the wicked die their spirits return to earth in the body of a bear. Others deny this but few of them will touch a bear. Remember that you are never to do so."

On our last trip to the Issue House the butcher had given Grandmother the head of a beef. She dug a pit and burned wood to coals in it. Upon them she heaped grass and then the head, face down. She covered all with earth, tamped it down and left it overnight. When she took the head from the pit she peeled the skin off. The meat was almost as tender as jelly and had about the same consistency. It was delicious. I thought I had never eaten better meat. Now I was never to partake of the meat from an animal's head again. I was puzzled by this and about the bears also.

Grandmother had told me stories of bears, but always of kind things they had done for people. One had befriended a woman who was lost and in her wanderings climbed toward the crest of a steep ridge. She had almost reached the top when suddenly a bear stood erect in her path. She fled to the left, circled a clump of junipers, and was again confronted by it. She turned back to the right, went some distance beyond her original trail and climbed to the summit. From it she saw Mexican soldiers camped at the foot. Had she not been diverted she would surely have been seen and captured.

"Then the bear was her friend?"

"It seems so. She had Power over bears; I knew a man who had it also. He trained one to hunt with him. Bishi and the bear could talk with each other, just as all Apaches could in the beginning when men, animals, and plants all spoke the same language. This bear helped Bishi kill game and ate only the parts given for his share. When they got close to camp the bear would say, 'Now, take the meat from my back for I cannot go closer or people will say you are a witch.' "

"What are witches, Grandmother?"

"People like ourselves, but people who have Power. They can be either men or women. It is difficult to explain, even difficult to understand. They use their Power for evil instead of good. They are very dangerous and to be avoided. Never have any association with witches, little son."

I promised.

"Loco was attacked by a bear once; it bit out a chunk of his leg, and he has been slightly crippled since."

"Did it put out his eye?"

"No; but it injured his eye and scarred his face."[1]

"Do witches do that?"

"No. But they do all sorts of bad things. They cause troubles to come to those they dislike, and especially to their children. Some think it is done with the eyes, as owls do. Some use crude dolls; they cut off the head or shoot arrows into the body of the doll; then their victim is wounded in the same place as the doll. If Apaches find a person guilty of witchcraft they banish him. That is the worst punishment one can suffer — worse than death — to leave one's people, never to return."

Regardless of stories to the contrary, our people did not condemn without a trial conducted by the chief. Liars were not permitted to give testimony. If the individual was found guilty, the wronged man became the executioner. The condemned had the option of defending himself, but if he killed his accuser, the next of kin challenged him to a duel with knives. Sometimes, in less serious cases, settlements were made with horses or blankets.

A banished person could not take refuge with another tribe, but sometimes found others of his kind with whom he banded together. These owed allegiance to no chief and took orders from no one. Such bands sometimes brought condemnation on a tribe by attacking travelers across the land of a leader who normally prevented his own men from such deeds. They attacked travelers not only to secure ammunition but to flout the authority of their former chiefs and to bring trouble to the people who had banished them.

•   •   •

Victorio had scrupulously preserved peaceful relations with the people of Monticello. In return they obtained ammunition for him and exchanged food and calico for meat and hides. They supplied him also with coffee, which our people liked.

Once when Nana had taken my mother and me to the trading post, the owner had given me white sticks striped with red, sweet and delicious. He gave me three but I saved two for Grandmother and Siki. While I munched, the trader told Grandfather of an attack made upon him and his small son only three days before. They had gone out to round up their cattle and been sighted by a band of seven outlaw Apaches. These men had ridden to cut off their return to the village. The trader had called to them, *"Victorio! Capitán Victorio, mi amigo!"* They had wheeled and ridden away.

Grandfather sent me back with the women, and with his men took the trail of the renegades. They knew well how to cover it; but there was no more expert trailer than Nana. He followed for three days and surprised them at a cache that Grandfather thought known only to himself.

The seven men were disarmed and bound. They did not deny that they were witches but boasted of their Powers and threatened Grandfather with disaster. One of them even had the courage to remind Grandfather that Blanco had told the Warm Springs Apaches what Child of the Waters had commanded: if an enemy lay down his arms his life was to be spared. Nana gave each an opportunity to speak. Six boasted of the evil they had done. The last to speak told Grandfather that if they were killed their ghosts would return to haunt him. The seventh was a young boy who had made no attempt to defend himself.

"Speak!" ordered Nana. The lad arose, held himself erect and looked Grandfather steadily in the eye.

"I have no Power," he said. "These men captured me and have

held me by force. They took my horse and my weapons. They forced me to care for their horses and to cook for them."

"You could not escape?"

"I could not. But I am an Apache and know how to die."

With his nose Nana indicated the horses. "Select the one you prefer, and saddle it. Mount and ride with me."

He nodded to his warriors and with the boy beside him rode slowly up the hill. At the top they halted. Wisps of smoke curled from the canyon, but there were no cries, no shots. They waited until the warriors joined them and rode away.

Rolled in my blanket by the fire I thought much. Blanco would have forbidden this thing, but Grandfather had not. And there was no one kinder than he. It was very puzzling.

It was not long before I had cause to know that Grandfather had been justified in his punishment of witches. One evening Victorio and his men rode in from a raid. I ran with the older boys to take their horses. The chief dismounted as though very weary and ignored the eager hands outstretched for his reins. Kaytennae took his horse and Victorio walked to Grandmother's shelter. He dropped beside the fire and said, "My sister, I bring bad news. Call your daughter."

When Mother came from the arbor he stood before her and said, "Meet this thing bravely as your husband would wish you to do. He is dead. Let his name be unspoken henceforth."

Dead! My father!

Mother bowed her head and pulled her blanket over her head. She returned to the arbor and seated herself. For a long time she was silent, motionless. Then she took her knife from her belt and cut her hair short to the shoulders. Grandmother set about preparing food for the men. Victorio talked briefly with Nana and retired to the shelter kept for his use. We did not see him again till morning. People spoke quietly to Nana and Grandmother but no one approached my mother. Grandmother gave me food and took me to Nana. I looked for Grandfather Sánchez, but he was not among the men. Suldeen told us what had happened:

Three Mescaleros had accompanied them on the raid. There was one of them who was suspected of wielding evil Power, but there was no proof. The men avoided him, even the other Mescaleros, but did not mistreat him. My father treated him kindly though Grandfather Sánchez attempted to warn him. Because there was no evidence of the evil one's guilt, they could do nothing but watch. They were in the Florida Mountains south of Deming when troops appeared, troops led by Yuma Apache scouts. My father, Kaytennae, and Nana's son were hidden near each other behind a little knoll, facing the soldiers. Suddenly shots were fired from the direction in which their own men were hidden and Nana's son died first. My father lived long enough to tell Kaytennae that he saw the Mescalero fire at him. Then he died.

Victorio had ridden his great white stallion to a ridge in an effort to draw the fire of the cavalry from the three men, but it was not the cavalry who had fired the shots. The three men took aim at the chief and killed his horse beneath him. Then the warriors had opened fire on the cavalry and routed them. They fled toward Fort Cummings. Victorio stayed long enough to give the slain men burial, and started in pursuit. The three Mescaleros stayed with the band because they knew that if one left it would be an acknowledgment of guilt. When they had chased the cavalry to the fort they turned east toward the Río Bravo.

As next of kin Sánchez was obliged to avenge the death of his son. Since one man had done the killing Sánchez would be avenging also the death of Nana's son. He had questioned Kaytennae as to the identity of the man but my father told only that it was a Mescalero — he had been unable to speak again. Sánchez suspected that the guilty man would attempt to slip away from the rest and escape toward morning before the rest awakened. Sánchez adjusted his own sleeping schedule so that he would be awake very early. He arranged with Victorio that the horses be placed some distance from the camp — farther away than usual, and that only our own men should conceal them. The Mescaleros knew they were under suspicion and did not protest. All kept their saddles in camp.

For several nights no sounds aroused my grandfather. Finally, in the dark of the moon, he heard stealthy movements. He suspected that the witch was stealing from the camp and watched him slip away stealthily. Sánchez took his rifle and went straight to the horses. He concealed himself and waited. It was some time before he detected the Mescalero approaching. He had not attempted to bring his saddle, but meant to ride away bareback. The Mescalero took his time. He did not mount the horse immediately but led it slowly from the arroyo. Sánchez followed, stopping when the horse stopped, moving when it moved. He knew that when the Mescalero thought it safe, he would mount and ride fast. As the man threw himself upon his steed a bullet found its mark. Holding to the mane the witch slipped slowly to the earth. Sánchez wanted him to know his executioner and did not fire again. Instead he bent over the dying man.

The Mescalero recognized him.

"Don't forget that your time, too, will come. May it be soon!" said the witch. And he died.

"Enjuh!" said Grandfather Nana.

"Enjuh!" said the rest.

• • •

Neither Mother nor Grandmother seemed greatly interested in me, and I was very lonely. Mother had been indifferent to all around her since she had ceased to go on raids with my father. After his death she seemed strangely apart. I was very much alone, without even a toy. I thought it would be wonderful to have a pet of some kind and especially a dog. I asked Grandmother if she thought I might not get one. She seemed to understand my need for it.

"Not a dog, my son, but something much better, and soon."

"Is anything better than a dog?"

"Wait and see. I believe you will think so."

One morning Grandmother placed something in my arms, something wrapped in a piece of blanket. It squirmed and whimpered. Mother smiled at me for the first time in days. But it was Grandmother who said, "You have a little sister, Torres."

The Warpath

The warriors had come and gone without ever having been enrolled at the agency. Victorio, Kaytennae, and three others went to the new agent, Mr. Russell, and were promised rations. They were promised also that the families of the men who wished to live on the Mescalero Reservation would be brought from San Carlos. Some of the women of Nana's band had been captured and taken to the Gila with Loco's people, and they were to be returned. Mr. Russell said that it might even be possible to bring Loco's band, at least those who wished to come.

Victorio and his men selected a campsite from which they could easily escape if it should become necessary. He knew that the Mescaleros trusted Dr. Joseph C. Blazer, a dentist who had bought the only lumber mill in that area, so he camped across the Tularosa from Blazer's Mill with the mountains at his back. He went to the trading post and the dentist received him kindly. Victorio bought food to last until Issue Day; after Saturday he expected to be given food with the rest. When the Mescaleros came, Victorio waited courteously until both they and the enrolled Warm Springs Apaches had received their portions. Then he presented himself at the window. The man in charge spoke Spanish and had no difficulty in explaining to Victorio that he was forbidden to distribute food without a ration card. The chief had no card—only the promise of the agent. Victorio went

[61]

to Mr. Russell who pretended to be busy with papers. For some time he ignored Victorio. No Indian was ever so ignorant as to misunderstand the insolence of this gesture. Victorio addressed him in Spanish, which the agent did not speak. Then Victorio asked José Carillo, the interpreter, to tell the agent he had been refused food until he could produce a ration card. Mr. Russell replied that he could not issue one without approval from Washington. Mail was slow—it might be a month.

Victorio bade José tell the agent that a month is a long time to be without food. Upon receiving no reply he went again to Dr. Blazer.

"You see, chief, Mr. Russell is new; he is trying to obey orders to the letter. I believe he is honest and means well. Meanwhile you need not lack for food. I have fat cattle in the corral. Kill one. Take what food you need from the shelves. And be patient with the agent. Think what your people face if you leave the reservation with them."

"He promised food and refused to give it," said the chief. "It was not to be a gift, but a payment made by the government for taking our reservation, and for our preserving peace."

"Yes, I know. But the cavalry has orders to kill all found off the reservation. You'll be killed."

"We'll not be killed. We'll be free. What is life if we are imprisoned like cattle in a corral? We have been a wild, free people, free to come and go as we wished. How can we be caged?"

"In time, word will come and you will get food. I believe it is to your interest to wait."

Magoosh, chief of the Lipans, entered the store. He had brought his people for refuge just as Nana had. He, too, urged the chief to wait.

"If you take your people and leave, where will you go?" he asked.

"To Juh's stronghold in the Sierra Madre."

"I know the Blue Mountains, but not the retreat of Juh."*

"Few do. Juh is my friend; I have visited him there. He married the sister of Geronimo, and we can count on their support. Our combined forces could control Sonora. We do not fear Mexican cavalry. They are taken from prisons and forced into the army. They can never reach the mountain upon which Juh lives, and we could

---

*Blue Mountains was the Apache name for the Sierra Madre.

live as our fathers did in the old days before the coming of the White Eyes."

"That would be good," said Magoosh.

"But I prefer my own country and hope to get it back," said Victorio.

The Lipan chief shook his head.

"Already there is cavalry in Soldier Canyon," he said.

"Sent to capture us," replied Chief Victorio.

"Roman Chiquito has forbidden his warriors to join you if you take your people to Mexico," said Magoosh.

"And Natzili?"

"His sympathy is with you, but he asks what is to be gained by leaving comparative safety for the certainty of war."

"And you, my brother?"

Magoosh was silent for a few minutes. Then he said, "I know Mexico well. I do not know what my people would do. You know they make decisions themselves as to war. I think some of them would go."

For two or three days the situation remained unchanged. Dr. Blazer attempted to placate the chief and to prevent his leaving. Blazer told the Warm Springs people that in New Mexico warrants for the arrest of Victorio had been issued, that a bounty had been placed upon the heads of his people, but that the cavalry were not there for the purpose of arresting them. Then rumors came of troops moving from the Pecos through the valley of the Peñasco. Fort Stanton was very close. So near were the troops in Soldier Canyon that Victorio could hear the bugle calls.

Again he went to the agent.

"Does your word mean nothing?" he asked.

"I am your friend," was the reply.

"Does a friend refuse food to a friend?"

The agent turned to his desk and picked up some papers. He could hardly have done a more irritating thing. Kaytennae looked at his chief and Victorio nodded. The young man grabbed the agent's long beard and dragged him about his office, the agent all the while imploring the interpreter to "talk pretty" to Victorio. José Carillo was thoroughly enjoying the spectacle, and not until Kaytennae had kicked the agent out of his own office did José convey the message.[1]

Shortly before sunset troops rode down to purchase some of Dr. Blazer's hay for their horses. Victorio saw them, and he heard the bugle. He and his men ran away from the camp. On the twenty-first of August, 1879, Mr. Russell reported to General Hatch that the Warm Springs band had left the reservation, probably to intercept the families believed to be en route from San Carlos to Mescalero. They had gone by Three Rivers toward the San Andres, and he judged them to be seventy-five or eighty miles west of Fort Stanton. In September Russell quoted Colonel Torrington as saying that a thousand soldiers could not have kept the Warm Springs on the reservation.

That Russell was an agent only, shows in his correspondence: "Have just received a letter from Lt. Col. N.A.M. Dudley, Commander Fort Stanton, informing me that a subordinate is instructed to arrest the Ojo Caliente Indians at this Agency and take them to Fort Stanton. Please instruct me at once how to act."

On July 5, Agent Russell had reported that three indictments for horse stealing and one for murder had been found against Victorio in Grants County, New Mexico. He said, "There is little if any doubt but an effort will be made to arrest him . . . I respectfully ask instructions as to my duty in case an effort is made by civil authorities to arrest Victorio."

Russell wrote to General Hatch that the Warm Springs people had left the reservation and said, "While I am satisfied that there is not a more turbulent tribe of Indians in the United States than the Warm Springs Apaches I frankly admit my disappointment and regret this escapade."

He said also, "There are as many killed by Americans and Mexicans as by Indians, but everything that happens is charged to the Indians. . . . Why let them learn that the cavalry can't catch them?"

It was entirely unnecessary to attempt to keep that information from Victorio. He had long been aware of it. The military officers were, also. When had an officer ever reported capturing a warrior? How many warriors had they killed? Was it not women and children they captured?

•   •   •

I well remember that mad flight from the reservation. I rode behind Grandmother, followed by Mother with little Chenleh in a *tsach* (cradle) on her back. We took everything that could be

In all kinds of work and activity, even in flight from the enemy, Apache babies rode in a *tsach* or cradle on the mother's back.

packed on the horses, went over the saddle and down the west slope of the White Mountain, taking the trail between the White Sands and the Malpais toward the San Andres. With us were a number of Mescaleros, Lipans, and a Comanche. Victorio knew well that there were cavalry scouring the Tularosa Basin for us, and he did not let us stop except for short intervals until we reached the Sacred Mountain. There at our old camping place we rested and slept.

I remember most vividly our reaching a spring and not being permitted to drink. Both people and horses were jaded and thirsty. At such times, if there is insufficient water for both, the horses must drink, for without horses, escape is impossible. In this case there was plenty of water but Nana tasted it and forbade its use. It seemed a long time before Grandmother lifted me from her horse and gave me a very small amount of cold, sweet water.[2]

How long we remained in that retreat I do not know. We crossed the Río Grande without encountering troops and took refuge in the Black Range of our homeland. As much as possible families kept together. Blanco's wife and Siki were with us. My people had rigid rules of conduct affecting young girls, and the two stayed close to Grandmother. Occasionally the men of our family joined us, Blanco more often than Nana. When Grandfather slept I do not know. I think that three or four hours sleep a night served him, and a handful of jerky satisfied his hunger. People said that on the long trips he slept in the saddle.

Grandfather took us to a cave in the mountains and left us. There was food and other supplies, and water was available nearby. We lived unmolested for several weeks, gathering all the food in the vicinity. Mother killed deer and the women tanned the hides and made moccasins. They cut meat into thin strips, not across, but with the grain, and dried it. They made dresses from a bolt of calico cached in the cave. And they used the cooking pots left there, made of clay, undecorated, and with a semicircular base so perfectly balanced that they righted themselves if tipped.

Mother renewed Chenleh's cradle with clean soft buckskin. The *tsach* was made of split boughs, cut thin and scraped until they were smooth. A long, willow withe was bent to an elongated loop and the ends securely fastened to form the bed of the cradle. At the head another loop jutted out to form a projection—a roof to protect the baby from rain, sunlight, and insects. This was covered with buckskin, over which a cloth could be laid for additional protection. At the foot was a little platform that could be lowered for the growing child.

Along the sides buckskin was fastened for the purpose of holding the baby firmly to the cradle, regardless of position. These buckskin flaps were laced together after the unclad child was placed on one thick layer of soft, fine grass and covered with another. The grass could be discarded and replaced with more. When Mother could not heat water for bathing my little sister she warmed it in her mouth and let it dribble over the little body.

In cold weather a beautifully tanned wildcat skin was used for warmth. In warm weather the arms were free. Perhaps no more useful nor comfortable article for the care of an infant has ever been devised than the *tsach*. By placing the strap attached to it about her forehead or shoulders the mother freed her hands for rein or rifle. She could suspend the cradle from the limb of a tree or the horn of the saddle. She could stand it up or lay it flat. Always the baby was comfortable and protected.

When it was necessary to bathe Chenleh Mother would send me away on an errand. My people were very modest and respected the privacy of others. But when Chenleh was ready to be replaced in her cradle Mother sometimes wrapped her in a blanket and let me hold her. I loved the baby dearly and shall never forget how happy I was when she first extended her little arms to me. She was a strong, healthy, little thing. Even on the long, hard trips she seldom cried.

I was not yet old enough to be forbidden to talk face to face with my cousin, Siki. If cousins of the opposite sex conversed it was with an intervening screen of some kind, usually a bush and they talked with their backs toward each other. Until late years our churches kept curtains down the center aisle so that privacy could be maintained during the service. This plan served also to protect a man from seeing his mother-in-law and vice versa. These customs are no longer observed to any great extent, and no doubt they seem absurd to White Eyes. This I can say for them; they resulted in a womanhood noted for chastity.

It was in this mountain retreat that Grandmother told me the stories of our origin and religion. They are difficult for me to explain, though in many respects they parallel the stories of both the Old and New Testaments. I know this because of serving many years as interpreter for the Dutch Reformed Church at Fort Sill and having been a member of that church over sixty years.

Literally the meaning of Ussen is Creator of Life. As nearly as I can judge, our concept of Him is much like the ancient Hebrews' Jehovah. Let it be remembered that I am not informed on comparative religions, and am not greatly concerned with their differences.

We have a tradition of a Sacred Woman, called in our tongue, *Ish son nah glash eh*. Translation of this word is difficult. The first two syllables mean "woman"; glash is a powdered white chalk used in painting the dancers, and hence sacred. If the remaining syllables had any special meaning, it may have been lost in the changes every language undergoes. The name has been interpreted as White Painted Woman — not its exact meaning — but as close as I can get. I shall use that term because it is accepted and understood.

From earliest youth I knew of White Painted Woman and her Son, Child of the Waters. She was a woman of beauty and chastity. All men admired her but she refused to marry. A prolonged drought brought on a famine and many perished of hunger. As long as she had food she shared it. But a time came when without the miracle of rain nobody could survive. There was a legend that the people might be saved by a virgin willing to sacrifice her life to save theirs. White Painted Woman decided to make that sacrifice. She went from her people and lay upon a rock awaiting death. In the night rain fell upon her and a child was conceived. Because He had no earthly father, people called Him Child of the Waters for He was the Son of Ussen.

The story is not always told the same; some versions say that there had been other children but that a monster had devoured them. All agree that this Child was sacred. White Painted Woman had constantly to protect Him from the attempts of the terrible *Yehyeh* that sought His death. She dug a secret place and built a fire over the entrance. When danger threatened she hid the Child in this cave. When it was safe, she let him out to exercise.

The *Yehyeh* was said to have human form and to be of great stature. It destroyed the human race until only White Painted Woman and her Son were left. It did not kill her because it wanted her to produce more children for its food. Though the *Yehyeh* was not sure of the Child's existence he suspected it for he saw little footprints about the camp. He accused White Painted Woman of concealing her child from him. She knelt and with her closed fist made an imprint in the dust to which with her finger tips she added five tiny toes. Though she had made a very good imitation of a child's track the *Yehyeh* was not convinced. Had she not possessed great Power she would surely have lost her life.

The Child grew old enough to hunt. White Painted Woman made weapons for Him. He provided his mother with meat. Once He killed a deer, made a fire, and cooked some of the meat. The *Yehyeh* smelled the good odor and came to the fire. Though the monster was terrible the Boy did not fear him. The *Yehyeh* towered above the Child and roared, "What you have cooked is mine. Give it to Me."

The Boy faced him and said, "It is not yours; it is for me."

The *Yehyeh* took the meat from the coals.

The Boy replaced it on the fire.

"You're nothing but a boy; you can't fight me. Your weapons would do me no harm."

Child of the Waters replied, "You don't know what weapons I have, nor what harm I can do. You do not know My Power."

The *Yehyeh* sneered, "You'll fight me for the meat, then?"

"I will," stoutly answered the Child.

"Then stand away from the fire and we will fight."

The Boy stood firmly beside the meat and faced the monster. "Choose your weapons," He said. "Each is to have four shots; you may take the first."

The *Yehyeh* used a pine pole for the shaft of his arrows. Upon his chest he had four coats of stone. The Boy wore only breech clout and moccasins. His bow was small, and for arrows He used shafts of gramma grass. He held them at His side and faced His enemy.

The *Yehyeh* took careful aim and loosed his arrow.

"Whoosh!" said the Child, throwing up His arms. A very strange thing happened: the huge arrow shattered in mid-air and fell to the ground. Not even a splinter touched the Boy.

"Now it is My turn."

The Child fitted the grass stalk to His little bow, took careful aim, and fired. The missile struck the monster's chest and shattered the outer layer of stone so that it fell to the earth.

The *Yehyeh* fired three more shafts without touching the Child. Each of the Boy's shots took effect until only one coat of stone remained. It was transparent, and through it the Lad could see the pounding of the monster's heart. He knew that the *Yehyeh* was frightened. He took careful aim and with His gramma grass arrow penetrated both the stone and the heart of the wicked monster.

Thus did the Son of Ussen conquer the enemy of mankind. He lived long and taught good and the use of good things to the Apaches, all of whom are descended from Him. He told them to live at peace with their neighbors. They were not to fight unless attacked, but, if attacked, He bade them protect themselves. He told them that if an enemy laid down his arms his life was to be spared.

He taught them the use of herbs, and of Power, for health and protection.

The story says that Ussen was not convinced that the Child was truly His son. White Painted Woman only smiled, for she knew. Ussen made a test of Child of the Waters. He told the Boy to stand far away, and He hurled a thunderbolt at Him. When it turned harmlessly aside Ussen turned to the Mother. "This is truly my Son," He said. "And you are a true and worthy Mother."

After the Boy left her, White Painted Woman was given the wings of an eagle, and she flew to a mountain top, and that is our Sacred Mountain.

She was not seen again.

$\mathcal{T}$he Hunted

After the break from the Mescalero Reservation we were constantly harassed, not only by the Blue Coats but by prospectors and miners, ranchers, and cowboys. But the later weeks we lay concealed in the Black Range, afforded a sense of security we were not to experience again for more than two years. We lived in constant expectation of attack, and kept our meager equipment in readiness for flight. Each night the horses were hobbled in a hidden arroyo. Each morning the emergency rations were checked, and the blankets rolled.

The men of our family came when they could, to bring food and ammunition. Grandmother wished to go with Nana but he felt that until Chenleh was older it could not be. When he took my little sister in his arms no one could have believed him to be the fiercest and most implacable of all Apaches, but that was the verdict of my people. Certainly he was considered the shrewdest in military strategy, surpassing Victorio himself. We believed his ability to be the gift of his Power, but he made no such claim. No young warrior excelled him in endurance, and at that time neither his age nor his broken foot seemed to handicap him.

In September of 1879, Victorio, supposedly in Mexico, raided the cavalry at Ojo Caliente. The officers, with Negro soldiers, were at our old adobe building, across the Cañada Alamosa from Warm

Springs. The chief stationed men on the cliffs to roll rocks upon pursuers before dashing through the water gap and stampeding the horses down the river. As Victorio had hoped, not a shot was fired. Those who attempted pursuit were stopped by a shower of rocks. No living target was visible; not a warrior got a scratch. The cavalry did not have enough mounts to follow.

A week or so later the chief achieved a similar victory over a group of civilians north of Ojo Caliente on the Percha. He made a swift attack, and a swift retreat. Several White Eyes were killed and not a single warrior wounded. Colonel Dudley went in pursuit of our chief. Victorio chose the place of combat carefully. With boulders for protection and a mountain at his back, he let a few men be seen to lure the cavalry to attack. The officers should have known it was a trap, for they had been the victims of ambush many times. But they took the bait and were driven back. Dudley waited for reinforcements, and this merely gave more of Victorio's men time to join their chief.

When the attack began, Victorio, as was his custom, killed the horses first. Without exposing themselves to fire, the men waited their chances before risking bullets, and throughout the day killed the soldiers. All who ventured within easy range were killed. The rest hid until darkness and retreated.

The chief secured a few more mounts, a good store of ammunition, and the rations and clothing of the dead. Only shirts and ammunition belts were taken, for our men had no use for the other articles of dress. With his pack train, Victorio turned toward the Warm Spring, with cavalry at his heels. The rear guard kept up a continual fight, keeping far enough ahead and taking advantage of cover to pick off the soldiers as they advanced. They did not give the chief time to stop and cache any of his supplies. Like the quail that pretends to be wounded in order to lure pursuers away from his hidden family, the chief crossed the border into Mexico. The cavalry was at that time forbidden to cross the line and turned back.

Nana meanwhile came to our retreat. He took us and also a number of small bands who had been concealed as we had, and headed for the Big Bend country in Texas. There was less cover in those mountains, and fewer caches than in the Black Range and Mogollons. Victorio's object in going was to draw the cavalry from our old haunts. For weeks we fled from one range to another, crossing the open plains at night, with a strong advance guard preceding the women and children and warriors bringing up the rear. Children rode tied to horses and to adults.

Horses move long distances at a fast walk or a slow trot, not at the gallop. They can maintain a pace of five or six miles an hour half the night. When ours became exhausted we changed mounts, preferably to ranch horses roped out as we went. Our tired ones were loose-herded with us, or if we had had them long, they followed. Lozen was expert at roping, and she and the young boys picked up all the horses we encountered on our trips. No man in the tribe was more skillful in stealing horses or stampeding a herd than she.

It was a hard life, but we liked it better than the hopeless stagnation of the reservation and we were happier than at the Rinçonada. Again we had hope for freedom. Hardships imposed upon people are much more onerous than those they voluntarily assume.

I have read that Indians do not suffer as White Eyes do, that their nervous systems are less susceptible to pain. What utter nonsense! The difference lies in an attitude — a determination to endure without complaint. We were taught that from earliest recollection. Children rode behind grandmothers or in *tsachs* until the aged were forced to drop out and be left in secret retreats. If there were new babies sometimes these and their mothers were left. But the great majority kept on, with little food, with no fires, and often with terrible weakness and fatigue, but without complaint.

During those terrible times there was little mercy shown by either Indians or their enemies. The young officers have written honestly of their defeats, their inability to cope with Victorio, and their sufferings in pursuing him. They have admitted frankly that they were outwitted, out-maneuvered, and out-fought by a handful of ill-equipped, half-starved warriors, handicapped by the presence of their families, and dependent upon what they could steal of food and ammunition. They testified to the caliber of my people by placing thousands of theirs in the field against a few — a very few — of ours.

Both Nana and Kaytennae have said that Victorio's warriors never numbered more than seventy-five, and that the Mescaleros and Chiricahuas who joined him at times did not exceed half that. It was reported that "Caballero" and fifty Mescalero warriors joined us along the border, but the Warm Springs or Mescaleros did not know of this force, and neither did the agent at Mescalero. For that matter I have never found one person who ever heard of this Caballero. It is possible that the Indians knew of him by some other name.

In Mexico there were villages from which Victorio could obtain ammunition and food in return for protection. It was an equitable arrangement — advantageous to the villagers. We were resourceful in obtaining food. I think we subsisted where White Eyes would have died. No doubt we were less particular than people who seldom went without eating more than twelve hours. After twelve days a man eats what he can get, whether he be red or white. One thing White Eyes never learned — to detect the presence of water underground. Many perished, when by digging two or three feet they could have obtained water.

When we were near a Mexican village Victorio forbade his men to drink the *mescal* which the inhabitants invariably gave to Apaches who would get drunk and be murdered. Our chief had seen Juh's warriors so betrayed. *Tiswin,* an undistilled drink, made of corn, and about as strong as beer, was made by the women, but an excess of grain was so rare that it was not made often. In very large quantities it was intoxicating, but there was seldom enough for that. Nana supported Victorio in his opposition to the use of the fiery Mexican liquor, but Sánchez had lived long among Mexicans and learned to like mescal.

*A*mbush

When we went into Chihuahua, Victorio took about four hundred fifty people with him, seventy-five of them warriors. Many more were thought to have been with him, and the military officers believed these reports to be true. The men of my family think the reports were mistaken.

It is true that there were a few Mescaleros and Lipans with Victorio, but not fifty warriors. Some from Mescalero followed after Victorio left the reservation, and among these were Magoosh and Crook Neck. The latter was then seventeen years old. Magoosh took his family, and his son, Willie, was born in Mexico. I have interviewed many of the older people at Mescalero to ascertain how many went, and all think the number very small.

We were essentially a mountain people, moving from one chain to another, following the ridges as best we could. If there were no mountains we took cover in arroyos, but survival on the desert and plains was much more difficult. I think we may have invented trench warfare, and we infinitely preferred a mountain at our backs. I doubt that any people ever excelled us as mountain climbers. Scaling walls was taken for granted. When closely pursued we killed our horses and scaled cliffs no enemy could climb. Men tied ropes to women and children and lifted them from ledge to ledge until they could take cover or escape. If the women and children could go ahead the warriors picked off the scouts, who always preceded the cavalry. We moved at night only when forced to do so and never fought in the darkness unless attacked. There was a belief that he who kills at night must walk in darkness through the Place of the Dead. I cannot say that all Apaches believed this, but many did. Like White Eyes, we had skeptics among us.

On our way north, late the next summer expectations were for attack from the north or west, but Victorio heeded the warning. With his band he started toward a spring, well concealed and a retreat from the hardships of flight. It was in a canyon with steep slopes, and with many boulders on either side of the little stream. In that place we could hold off a superior force. Our people were weary and eager to rest. As we approached the mouth of the canyon, sure enough — dust in the east warned us of the approach of a big party. We had crossed the Río Grande into Texas, and had no cause to fear the Mexican cavalry. A scout came in to report that a wagon train was heading for our refuge. Victorio sent the women and children up the slopes to shelter, and stationed his men at the entrance of the gorge.

It was well that we had not gone on to the spring, for farther up, the Blue Coats lay in ambush waiting for us. The troops outnumbered us; they had fresh horses and much ammunition. They saw the wagon train approaching and dashed to its defense. There was nothing for the chief to do but take his weary people and depart. He started for the Río Grande. He knew the short cuts, the water holes, and the places adapted to defense. But he was encumbered with noncombatants, jaded horses, and weary people. They needed no orders to fall into the usual formation with the men protecting the rear. Knowing that concealment was impossible Victorio made straight for the border.

After we had topped the last ridge and the river was in sight Lozen came to Grandmother. With her was a young woman. The three turned from the line of march toward one of the infrequent thickets. Grandmother wanted to stay with them but Lozen forbade it.

"Take our horses," she said, "so that the soldiers will not know any have stopped. We will follow."

We rejoined the line of march leaving the two women unprotected, and without mounts. The soldiers followed us to the water's edge, but all had crossed and were out of range before they arrived. They turned back.

"They will ride slowly," said Grandmother, "and may find the tracks leading away from the trail."

It was long before we learned that the women had not been discovered. Victorio had said that Lozen, even without horses, was well able to protect herself and the young mother. She had a knife and blankets, her emergency food, her rifle, and cartridges. He said that no one was to wait for her, but that we were to scatter, for there was danger of the Mexican cavalry attacking us from the south.

We broke into small groups, spreading fanwise as we went. Kaytennae rode with Grandmother and me; Mother, Siki, and Blanco's wife followed. He took the route closest to the wagon road and followed it two days before turning east to meet a larger group. We rode north, avoiding bare ridges except when we had to cross one. In a mesquite thicket where we found a little water Kaytennae let us rest and build a fire of very dry wood. From the crest of a hill our lookout saw a coach coming north. He signalled Kaytennae, and two men rode out with him. We lay concealed and waited. We heard no shots, but in an hour or so the men returned with the equipage, drawn by two fine horses. Before it walked two men, a woman, and a little boy. All were dressed in the Mexican fashion — *ricos,* I think.

We needed horses badly but not prisoners. Kaytennae ordered that the men be taken down a little arroyo. I knew well what was in store for them, and they doubtless did, too, but they walked without protest before the warriors. I had seen death in many forms and took it for granted. I did think of Blanco's admonitions and wondered if he were present if he would sanction the shots that followed.

The woman stood motionless until she heard them. In the manner of her people she fell to her knees and with hands uplifted cried, *"Dios! Dios!"* over and over. Her little son ran to her; she drew him close and bent protectingly over him. I did not realize what was to happen until a stone struck her forehead and blood dripped upon the child. She fell forward, still shielding him. I ran into the mesquite thicket until Grandmother overtook me. She knelt, even as the woman had done, and took me in her arms.

She, too, was shaking. I had seen many deaths without so react-
ing, but I felt that this was cruel and unnecessary. I thought of the
two women we had left north of the *Río* and wondered if the soldiers
had treated them so.

There came the sound of people mounting horses and we joined
them. We could not reach them without passing that dreadful place
and I did not want to see it.

"There is only a pile of stones, Torres," said Grandmother. And
she lifted me behind her saddle.

Wanderings

Before I slept I heard Kaytennae deliver a message to Grandfather. A Mescalero hunting in the mountains brought word that the Blue Coats had crossed the border in search of us. Until that time we had been comparatively safe south of the Río Grande.

Before daybreak we rode. We divided into small parties each of which was to seek a different refuge. Each knew where and when it was to assemble and combine forces with those of Victorio. Kaytennae, Suldeen, Blanco and his younger brother whom we do not name, were sent with us. I think there may have been twenty-five including the four men.

We made various attempts to find a crossing unguarded but both Blue Coats and Mexican cavalry were scouting the river. I do not know just where we succeeded, but we spent one night near Hueco Tanks. It was a long ride to the Sacramentos with no water. But once in the mountains we had no difficulty except that of concealment. We made a leisurely trip north, with the men constantly watching the Tularosa Basin, a mile below us. Only when we found a deep side-canyon could we risk building a fire, and it was cold on the summit. Kaytennae took no chances with soldiers in the flat country. He and Suldeen went down the steep west slope until they reached a broad ledge overhanging a spring at the foot. From it they could see tiny

[79]

moving dots approaching. Scouts! They traveled fanwise ahead of the cavalry, usually miles ahead. As the dots increased in size Kaytennae recognized the scouts by the way they walked. They converged, to head toward the spring above which Kaytennae lay.

When General Crook first employed scouts to guide the cavalry it was against their enemies. Being chosen as scouts was a recognition of a warrior's ability to fight, and it was a relief from the dreary, monotonous existence on the reservation. To Apaches a reservation is a prison. Scouts were admired and envied by other men — not for the meager pay, for at that time money meant nothing to them. What they valued was the possession of a rifle and ammunition, for they had been deprived of arms when they went on the reservation. In addition Crook used the scouts against their enemies, the Pimas. The Chiricahua and Warm Springs had fought occasionally also with the Tontos, though they were Apaches. The name *Tonto,* meaning fool, was given them because they were considered inferior in intelligence. So scouts who fought against the Tontos were not despised by their own people.

Chihuahua, Tissnolthos, and Speckle Face were riding close, Chiricahua warriors wearing the red head-cord that was their badge of servitude. Good and true warriors inveigled into military service and now used against their own people! Those who attempted to leave the service were grimly informed of the punishment meted out to deserters. These three had gone to San Carlos with Cochise's band and found existence unendurable. Kaytennae's heart burned within him as he thought of how these men who should be fighting with him were the allies of his enemies.

They were cutting for sign before coming into the water. Not once did they look toward the ledge. He waited while they drank, one at a time, with the others keeping watch. When they had finished he was so enraged that he leaped to his feet and yelled, "Come up here!"

He had them covered.

"We'll give you metal, more than you want. I have sharp metal for your treacherous hearts. Brave warriors who fight their people deserve reward. We'll give it. Come!"

The scouts fled.

Suldeen reproved him. The cavalry would be warned and would prevent our crossing the basin to the Organs on its western edge.

Kaytennae admitted that he had been hasty, but reasoned that without water the cavalry would turn south to the Hueco Tanks or the Río Grande.

"And where will we cross the plain?"

"At Dog Canyon."

"It is a good place for those who wish to ambush the Blue Coats," said Suldeen. "I know that place well. There is a narrow, winding trail leading into it. The entrance is not very wide, and between it and the narrow gap a short distance back is a spring. Beyond it, the walls are so close together that only one horse at a time can pass, and to do so he must scramble up a waist-high ledge. For an enemy coming in from the basin it is a death trap. The Mescaleros, and Nana, too, have sent two or three out on the floor to lure cavalry into ambush. Once through that narrow opening with its perpendicular walls they can be killed with rocks from above.

"But to those leaving the canyon there is no protection. They must spend the night in it, for the descent cannot be made in the dark. The women and children must walk down, and the horses must be led by the men. We dare not risk going through the gap till morning. We should start as early as possible, for it is a hard trip across the basin, with little water."

We rode hard to the head of that trail for we knew the Blue Coats might return to intercept us. True, they might go on to Hueco Tanks, but there was also the probability of their making a dry camp or getting water beneath the ledge.

When I have nightmares I still descend that perilous trail. Only those who have attempted it, as it was then, can know how narrow and slippery was the footing. How Mother, with Chenleh on her back, made it safely I do not know. Before we slept, everything and everybody were at the floor of the canyon and in readiness for an early start. One man stood guard at the gap, and another at a sharp point on the trail.

We rode from between the sheltering walls into darkness and were well on our way across the floor of the basin before it was light. With Kaytennae scouting ahead and Blanco guarding the rear we headed toward three little peaks jutting up from the wide, sunken plain. We reached the peaks without sighting the enemy. Kaytennae had waited there for us, keeping watch in all directions. There were two young boys with us, and he stationed them to guard the southern approach. Siki was sent up the east slope to watch for pursuers from that direction.

There was a little trickle of water and it took a long time for people to drink and fill their jugs before watering the horses. They had not finished when Siki called to us that she saw moving objects bobbing up and down beyond the low ridge we had crossed an hour before. She thought they might be the heads of horses.

"Crows, more likely," said Blanco, "but watch closely while I get the boys. The rest will mount and follow Kaytennae. Call me if you see them again."

Mother, with Chenleh on her back, rode west after the others, but Grandmother and I waited with Siki's horse. Blanco, as rear guard, waited until she came running toward us. "Horses!" she gasped, "three, coming fast!"

We followed the rest, with Suldeen and his brother riding last. We had the advantage of a brief rest and water. If the scouts stopped at the little peaks they could pause very briefly and then be at our heels. The cavalry, if they waited to eat and water their horses, would be hours behind. We seldom had food oftener than morning and evening, and then sometimes we ate as we rode.

My people knew well how to get the most from a horse without running it to death. We took care to give our mounts every advantage. The Tularosa Basin is comparatively level till the foothills begin, and from there on the ascent is abrupt. We reached the foothills and concealed our steeds and ourselves among the boulders. With three men and Mother (an excellent shot), and a mountain at our backs, we waited for Kaytennae. We had not even seen him, and we knew that since the scouts were not trailing us, they must be after him. Toward sundown Blanco sent his young brother back to reconnoiter. He did not return until long after dark, but Kaytennae was riding behind him.

Kaytennae had sighted a buckboard drawn by two fine horses coming up the trail from El Paso. He knew the men had not seen him because they kept on their course. He left his horse in an arroyo and lay along the trail. It was over very quickly. As he was cutting a horse from the vehicle he saw the scouts between him and our band.

Kaytennae's horse was jaded, and he had killed the men to

obtain a fresh mount. Without waiting to get his saddle he sprang to the horse's back. Expert as he was he could not budge the animal. It balked. The scouts were riding hard. He prodded the reluctant steed with a knife but it refused to move. He ran to the arroyo and began crawling up it toward the mountain. When he found sufficient cover to conceal his head he saw, to his surprise, that the scouts had crossed the arroyo and were circling to the south. He knew that they would find his horse and trail him. Fortunately it was getting dark, and he left the shelter of the ditch and ran up the trail until he met the man who had gone in search of him.

All these men, like myself, were later prisoners of war for twenty-seven years. They went first to Florida, then Alabama, and later to Fort Sill. They were friends and enjoyed talking over their early experiences. I never tired of hearing their stories, and enjoyed this at Kaytennae's expense, though he was my stepfather. Years later, Tissnolthos, who was with Geronimo's band for awhile told of that chase with tears of laughter in his eyes:

"We were miles ahead of the cavalry, as usual, for they weren't in any hurry to catch up with any Apaches, even women and children. The soldiers would never know what we did, and besides, Kaytennae was my relative. Speckle Face, too. Do you think we wanted to kill Kaytennae? We were laughing till we almost fell off our horses. He had talked so bravely from the ledge when he had the drop on us that we wanted to turn the tables on him. He had caused us to go a day and a night without water.[1]

"We knew, too, that he'd follow you, and thought it served him right to have to walk."

Kaytennae smiled and made no comment.

Tissnolthos continued: "We crossed the pass and went down the long slope toward the Río Bravo; then we turned north on the Jornada del Muerto until we were opposite the spring at the foot of the Sacred Mountain.

Kaytennae took up the narrative: "That place had many times afforded refuge to us and our people. We spent the night at Grandmother's old camp and she told me of how we had lain in hiding when cavalry came in from Fort Stanton and attempted to reach the

Elders of the Warm Springs tribe, many of them participants in this story, added their own reminiscences to the narrator's records. From the top (left to right): Martine, Eugene Chihuahua, David Belen, Guydelkon, Kayitah; second row: Kinzhuma, Estoni, Blind Tom, Tissnolthos, Kuni; bottom row: Kaizah, Chato, Sam Kenoi, an unidentified Anglo, Rogers Toklanni, Charles Istee.

spring. On a ledge above it, Victorio had stationed warriors to command the approach. The cavalry had drunk the water Nana had forbidden us to touch, and so had their horses. Both had become ill from a laxative effect, and were weakened until they could hardly travel. We had not poisoned that spring; the illness was caused by a natural mineral that this one time operated in our favor.

The troops were easily beaten back until more cavalry came in from the Tularosa Basin. Nana took the women and children up the arroyo and around a point to the Jornada. The trail was very rocky and there was little dust to warn us of the coming of an enemy until they were almost upon us. As the cavalry rounded a point of rocks pretty well lined with mesquite, Grandfather sent the people east, following a rocky ledge, to the shelter of an arroyo. While they were concealing themselves and their horses the boys hastily did what they could to cover our trail. Fortunately, unshod hoofs make little noise and leave few traces of their passing. Taking advantage of every clump of vegetation, every rock, our people stood with hands ready to press the nostrils of our horses so that they would not betray our position. Mother took off Chenleh's cradle and handed it to Grandmother, freeing her to use her rifle. If the baby had opened her mouth to make a sound it would have been necessary to smother her cries, for the ears of scouts are good.

There we waited anxiously until the scouts had passed. I think we could not have been more than a quarter of a mile off the trail, and it seems impossible that our presence was not detected. Not one even glanced in our direction. It was not long before the Blue Coats came into sight. It was a very large detachment, several companies. We learned later that it was commanded by Colonel Hatch, and that he had been sent to cut off our retreat. Nana did not wait long in hiding. He anticipated that the cavalry would follow Victorio, and that our band, being of less importance, might be of secondary interest. Over the Jornada we rushed, that trail which my people had made a terror to invaders. After a long ride the line stopped. Men broke the lock at the well, drew water in a bucket, and we drank. When the horses had finished we mounted again. I do not remember having crossed the Río Bravo, for I slept much of the time. I think we got no real rest until we were in a canyon of the Black Range. If, as people believed, Grandfather could sleep in the saddle, it could not have been very satisfying sleep. When we reached the cave in the Floridas two or three weeks later he really rested for two days. Kaytennae stood guard, and Grandfather was aroused only when a runner came to report cavalry in the vicinity.

In that cave Nana had previously cached food and supplies. I remember great stacks of cotton cloth from which the women made dresses. Two pieces sewed together at the sides formed the skirt. Another long strip with a slit cut crosswise in the middle was worn by slipping the head through the aperture, and closing the seams under the arms. The women used a cactus thorn with the fiber attached for needle and thread. They made breech clouts for the men, and took with them a supply of muslin and calico for those who might need it.

After this came the dash to the border and the meeting with Victorio.

•   •   •

Kaytennae took his charges over almost that identical route. Grandmother pointed out to me the places where we had hidden, and the sites of our camps. We passed so close to Fort Cummings that we could hear the bugles. Kaytennae had learned that only a few soldiers remained within the walls, the rest being out scouting for us. He had, he said, watered his horse from the spring at the fort, but he would not risk that with the women along.

He was impatient to rejoin Victorio. The Blue Coats were cooperating with the Mexican cavalry in running us down, and the chief needed every warrior. He especially needed Kaytennae, who as a fighting man was unsurpassed.

We crossed into Mexico west of the river, by the old Smuggler's Trail, and turned southeast. We arrived at the rendezvous before Victorio did. To Grandmother's great disappointment Lozen was not with the warriors. With her present we had no fear of a surprise attack. With the Blue Coats in the field we needed her more than before. Because nobody spoke her name I knew that they thought her dead. When they referred to her it was as Victorio's sister, or the Medicine Woman.

As we rode Grandmother sang the prayer Lozen had always used in her rite of determining the direction of the enemy:

> In this world Ussen has Power;
> This Power He has granted me
> For the good of my people.
> This I see as one from a height
> Sees in every direction;
> This I feel as though I
> Held in my palms something that tingles.
> This Power is mine to use,
> But only for the good of my people.

"You know the prayer, Grandmother. Why don't you use it as she did?

"That is not permitted. It is the Power given her when we made her feast, the Power she had earned in her vigil on the Mountain. Nobody else can wield it."

"Could Siki? She made her feast not long ago."

"No, not Siki. She is but a child, my dead sister's child. She was given a Power — that of escaping from her enemies. But she cannot do what Victorio's sister can — no one else can."

"If Siki has the Power of escaping from her enemies why doesn't she get her father from San Carlos?"

"If she were with him she might. Loco went voluntarily, you know. Fortunately, Siki was not with him. He could not take a little girl on the warpath. He entrusted her to my care. I wish most sincerely that she could free her father, and I wish that she could take the Medicine Woman's place, but that is not to be."

$\mathcal{T}$res Castillos

In 1880, the Indian Moon [September] again shone upon us in the state of Chihuahua. We had assembled a day's journey southeast of the mountains at a place the Mexicans called Tres Castillos [Three Castles] because of the conformation.

One evening at Victorio's fire, before the men had gathered for the council, Victorio looked at me and spoke:

"Stand, my Son."

I obeyed my chief. He placed his hand upon my head and said, "Kaywaykla — His Enemies Lie Dead in Heaps. Let this boy be called by that name henceforth — Kaywaykla."

He left us.

"I am already Kaywaykla?"

"You are Kaywaykla. By the will of the chief you are Kaywaykla. Some day you also may be a chief, but not unless you fulfill the meaning of your name. Do not forget."

Erect as the chief himself, Nana strode to Victorio's fire. Grandmother brought food for the men, seated in a semicircle about him with only Grandfather's place vacant. When he sat down I crowded in between him and the chief. The men laughed and I knew I had done something amiss, but I was glad to hear the laughter. It had been lacking of late.

Mother set food and water before them and reached for me.

"Do not think that because your uncle has given you a warrior's name you can sit in the council."

"Let him stay," said the chief. "Already every child in the tribe knows how desperate is our situation."

Mother withdrew, but Grandmother remained seated behind Nana. I knew that Blanco was making medicine before he began blowing smoke toward each of the four directions. I could sense the solemn and reverent attitude of the men when Blanco rolled a cigarette in an oak leaf. The Council sat in silence until he finished. Our men did not smoke; nobody used a pipe. And only the medicine men could gather the herbs used in the ritual.

Victorio was speaking: "For a short time we may be comparatively safe here. The cavalry will look for us in the mountains, not on this plain. We need rest badly. We need food. Always, of course, our great need is ammunition. The warriors are away on a raid; some of them are hunting. Tonight three of them came in with thirty head of cattle. The rest will not return until they bring supplies.

"The cattle can be butchered tomorrow and the meat cut for drying. In two days of this sunshine, meat cut thin should be ready to pack.

"On the plain to the northwest, this side of Tres Castillos, there is a small lake and good grass. Between the lake and the ridges we can camp and prepare for the long and difficult journey west across the wide plains to the Blue Mountains. Once we reach the foothills of the range we will find ample food and many horses. There I have supplies of blankets, clothing, and ammunition, cached for just such an emergency as this. Before starting there we must prepare enough food for the ride. We may have to travel fast.

"What have you to suggest?" Victorio asked.

The men sat in respectful silence.

"Nana?"

"It is for my chief to say."

"I need the wise counsel of my father."

Nana was not Victorio's father, but his uncle. The term "father" was used to show the respect the chief had for him, for the Apache values respect above all else.

Nana spoke: "I have fought with three great chiefs of my people, Mangas Coloradas, Cochise, and Victorio. The problems confronting you are more difficult than either of the others had to meet. To the future of our people your decisions are of greater importance. Your wisdom has never failed us. Command and we obey."

"My father knows well that I do nothing for credit. I seek only the preservation of my people. Without your wise planning we would have been destroyed long ago. Never have we been in desperate need of ammunition that my father has not supplied it. Again we are almost without it. Speak, I ask."

Nana asked eagerly, "Will you permit me to take a few warriors and make a raid for it? And meet you at Tres Castillos?"

"It will entail great risk. Nearly all the men are away, and there are few left to protect the women and children. It is I who should take that risk."

"Which needs protection more, the warriors or the women?"

"My father is wise. We shall both remain with our people, one to serve in the advance guard, the other the rear.

"Select a warrior for leading the raid. He must be wise enough to take no unnecessary risks, but daring enough not to return empty-handed. Choose!"

"Blanco!" said Grandfather without hesitation.

"Blanco," voted each in turn.

"Then Blanco it is. He holds our lives in his hand. Select your men, Blanco, and notify them tonight to be ready to leave before dawn. Leave us and prepare to ride."

The chief sat in silence with the firelight illuminating his handsome, tragic face. He turned to Grandfather. "There will be only twenty men in camp. I will take the lead with half. You, Suldeen, Mangus, Eclode, and Kaytennae will form the rear guard. Some may be needed as runners. Those hunting are mostly Mescaleros who joined us. They will meet us at Tres Castillos. Yours is the place of greatest danger."

"Usually," Grandfather replied.

"*Enjuh*! The council is ended."

When we reached camp, Chenleh was creeping on a blanket. When she saw me she smiled and held out her little arms. I held her while Mother placed food before us. Before he ate, Grandfather took her from me and talked to her. She cooed in response and tugged at the beads about his neck. He took them off and slipped them over her head. The necklace dangled to her feet. The long white beads were made of the shin bones of the deer, and there were many,

many of them. They covered his chest as a breastplate would, and I had seen him wear them only once before. The baby grasped them and tried to put one in her mouth. Mother took the ornament and fastened the buckskin thong to the cradle, and covered it with baby grass.

The women, as always, checked the water jugs and food bags before sleeping. In addition to the large jug, Mother had some small ones for individual use. Grandfather had not eaten his meat and she prepared another dish for him. Into a wicker cup she put some herbs, poured hot water over them, and thickened the infusion with mesquite-bean meal. She handed the brew to him and he drank it unprotesting. Then she brought tallow and attempted to remove his moccasin and rub his stiff ankle. That he would not permit, but he smiled his appreciation and applied it himself.

For two days the whole camp was busy butchering the beef, cutting it into long thin strips, with the grain, and spreading them upon mesquite bushes to dry. Then they pounded it so that it would be compact, and they packed it in leather bags made of cowhide. No attempt was made at distribution other than filling the emergency ration bags that each carried on his belt. There was no bartering or selling of the necessities of life. That is perhaps part of the reason the Apache has had great difficulty in adjusting himself to the commercialism of civilized living.

Before dawn of the third day the camp was astir. Pack animals were laden, and put in charge of the older boys. Horses were saddled, blankets and bags tied firmly to saddle, and the line of march formed. Before we were mounted Victorio, with the advance guard, rode by us to take the lead. Grandmother waited until almost all the long line had passed before joining it because she always stayed as near Nana as she could. I think perhaps four hundred had gone before she pulled her mount into the line. As usual, I rode behind her; then she halted and motioned to Blanco's wife, Siki, and Mother to go ahead of her. Mother rode a sure-footed mule, and had the *tsach* on her back. Two of Nana's captive Mexican boys followed us. Grandmother's sturdy cavalry horse plodded steadily through the gray October morning. It was cold, and I slipped under the fold of the blanket about her shoulders and nestled against her warm back.

I do not know how long I slept, but some time I think, for I was awakened by being uncomfortably warm. I was thirsty, too, but I did not ask for water. No Apache child did. Parents, like Ussen, knew one's needs and supplied them at the proper time.

Already the sun was high and hot; the grass was short and thin. Mesquite and cactus clumps were scattered over the plain; and in the distance everything shimmered. The horses plodded along, with vegetation becoming more scattered and stones more frequent. They gradually gave way to bare sand and a few big stretches of flat rock. At their edges were queer-looking holes and I asked what they were.

"The homes of rattlesnakes, Kaywaykla."

"Where are the snakes?"

"Deep in the earth where it is cool. They come out in the dark to hunt food. It is fortunate that we did not have to make this trip by night. Horses might have been bitten."

"Grandfather has the Power over them."

"He cannot prevent them from biting."

"Do the bites cause death?"

"Unless Grandfather cures the one bitten. Even then he suffers a long time and is very sick."

I had heard of sickness but had seen none. The soldiers and the horses who drank from the spring on the Malpais were sick. Our people did not have the illnesses of the White Eyes, except smallpox which I had never known. None of the so-called children's diseases, none of the common colds, none of the social diseases were then known to my people. Those were to come, along with other "blessings" of civilization.

It was past midday, and we had stopped once to drink from our jugs. Mother had released little Chenleh from her *tsach* and bathed her before lacing her into it again. She slept much of the time, her little head bobbing with the motion of the horse. Several times she opened her eyes and smiled at me. Not once did she cry.

The shadows to our right were long and grotesque before I got a glimpse of the low ridges ahead. To the south of them was a long sand dune, ending near the long slope leading up the east side to a bench on the mountain. It was bare, though above and below it there was vegetation among the boulders. Grandmother explained that beyond the dune was the lake, and between it and the foot of the mountain a grassy plain where we could camp and rest. We would build fires and cook food; we would rest by the good warmth and sleep undisturbed. Fires! Already the chill of evening made the idea welcome. Not long now . . . . .

The line ahead was swerving sharply to the left to circle the end of the dune and disappear behind it. I think the horses smelled the water for they began to step faster. Grandmother was talking of tall pines, mountain meadows, and clear, cool water in the land of Juh. A few more camps, a few more plains to cross, a few more days of attempting to avoid discovery, and we would find a refuge from White Eyes and their attack. We would dwell in a land such as our fathers had enjoyed, untouched by greed and cruelty. It would be like the Happy Place with no suffering, no injustice, no hunger.

"No death?" I asked.

"There will be death," said Grandmother, "but only when we are old and weary. It will come as the release to a better place."

We rounded the end of the dune and looked down upon a green meadow stretching to the lake. Already the men had unsaddled and their horses were drinking. People were making preparations for cooking and sleeping. I could see the flicker of flames on the shore, and the sparkle of water in a long glittering strip as the last rays of the sun shone upon the lake. Immediately ahead of us people pulled horses from the line of march as they found suitable camp grounds. Grandmother did not ride far into the meadow but stopped in a smooth grassy spot among the boulders, where there was dry wood at hand. She looked about and then moved up hill to a more sheltered position. A few stragglers were still coming in, but Grandfather and his men were probably a mile behind us.

Before unsaddling, Mother took Chenleh from her cradle and put her on a blanket spread upon the ground. She turned her back to me while she bathed the baby, wrapped her in a shawl, and placed her on the blanket. Siki sat her horse and took the reins as Blanco's wife and Grandmother unsaddled. I held the reins of mother's mount. The mule tugged to be released when Siki started toward the lake. My cousin stopped and waited to take him.

"Go on!" Mother called to her. "My mule will follow as soon as I get the saddle off."

Grandmother and Blanco's wife began gathering dry wood for a fire. The sun sank below the ridge and in the dark shadow of the evening it was chilly. I shivered with cold. When Mother came to take the mule I ran to my little sister and bent over her. She put up her arms, and I sat down and took her on my lap.

Then came the sound of shots! Many shots! Along the lake I saw flashes of fire. I put my sister on the blanket and ran to Mother.

"Indah! Indah!" [White Man] screamed Grandmother as she ran down the slope and started after Siki.

"Come back!" cried Mother, "Come back!"

Grandmother did not turn. She shook her head and continued her attempt to rescue my cousin.

Blanco's wife raced up the slope alone. Mother lifted me to my place behind the saddle and turned to get Chenleh. The mule was frightened and pulled away from the baby. Several times Mother got close, but each time she stooped, the frightened animal lunged and prevented her lifting Chenleh. People ahead raced back past us. A man called to Mother to mount and ride up the slope.

"Get my baby, Eclode," pleaded Mother. He nodded, stooped, and without stopping picked her up and ran on with her. When Mother saw that he did not intend bringing the baby to us she mounted and turned the mule toward the hillside. The first part of the ascent was easy. When we reached a little bench she stopped and we looked back at the lake where the flashes of fire were scattered and infrequent. We heard screams and shots. Horses galloped along the trail below us, horses with shod hoofs.

"The soldiers are riding to cut off escape to the mountains," she said. Then we heard the clank of metal on stone above us. Mother pulled her mount into the deep shadow of a boulder and stopped. The sounds came closer. She slid to the ground and pulled me down beside her. She headed the mule north and struck him sharply. He ran into the darkness. She turned again to the slope and we began climbing. We moved softly stopping occasionally to listen. I thought we were safe until I heard the sound of shod hoofs.

Mother heard it, too, and crept toward a huge boulder. When we reached it we found two huge rocks with tops touching and a narrow cleft between them. The entrance was very narrow. I thought of rattlesnakes, and drew back. Mother squeezed herself into the opening, sat down facing it and pulled me in after her. Without speaking I held back because I remembered the rattlesnakes. She pulled me down against her and we sat with her feet just inside the opening. More hoof sounds. Three riders halted close to our hiding place. I saw their rifles silhouetted against the sky.

Siki Toklanni, cousin of the narrator, was captured with her grandmother at Tres Castillos.

They spoke in Spanish. Then two rode away, but the third dismounted and led his horse straight toward us. I held my breath while he stopped and listened. He leaned his rifle against the rock within my reach, and stood there while he rolled and smoked a cigarette. I tried to still the beating of my heart. I could feel Mother's pounding at my back. Had I not been in the way she could have killed him with her knife, while he smoked. Finally he dropped his cigarette to the earth, ground his heel into it, and mounted.

When he was out of hearing we left our refuge and began crawling up the slope. There were still occasional shots behind us. Horses moved back and forth over the plain. That meant that our people were being hunted down and killed. But there were no cries. They were Apaches. I was out of breath though I had remembered to keep my mouth closed. Mother stopped and murmured, "We are close to the bench we saw, coming in. I have seen that place several times. There is a little dry arroyo crossing it. When we reach the bushes at this side we must crawl up the arroyo to the mountain. We must do it before the moon rises, and that will be very soon. Keep close."

In a clump of greasewood at the east edge of the bench we found a woman and a little girl.

"We have little time," said Mother softly, "Come!"

The woman replied, "Already it is too late. There are soldiers on both sides of the arroyo, some of them very close. We can not crawl through it without being seen."

"It is our only chance. One at a time we will start. I will send Kaywaykla first, let him get part way, and follow. You do the same; or go first if you wish."

The woman shook her head.

"Lie flat on your face, and feel ahead for cactus. When you stop, lie flat, but not long. Creep and freeze! When you reach the bushes on the other side wait for me."

I wriggled up the shallow ditch, not stopping till I heard something move. I listened. I started and a horse snorted. I knew that it had smelled me. I lay very still till I thought of the moon and that it would be up soon. I crept cautiously until I heard voices very close. I lay still. Then I felt ahead and twice moved a cholla out of my way. I got some thorns in my fingers but I went on. Many times I stopped before I saw a dark clump of vegetation and crept into its shelter.

Site of Tres Castillos Massacre

NEW MEXICO

● DEMING   ● LAS CRUCES

● HUECO TANKS

● EL PASO DEL NORTE

TEXAS

LAKE GUZMAN

TRES CASTILLOS   LAKE

DUNE

RIO GRANDE

● CASAS GRANDES

✖ SITE OF MASSACRE

ROUTE OF VICTORIO TO TRES CASTILLOS

MEXICO

RIO CONCHOS

CHIHUAHUA ●

When I looked back, the bright edge of the moon was lifting above the lake. I peered down the arroyo but could not see Mother. There was a bush in it, one that I had not passed. I could see and hear the soldiers plainly. Some had dismounted and squatted on the ground, others sat their horses, and nearly all were smoking. Moonlight was already touching the bench and shortly would flood it. I looked frantically for Mother, but saw nothing but the bush. It moved! It moved toward me. Then I understood. When it reached me Mother touched my lip with her fingers and we crept up the slope toward another dark spot. When we got among many clumps she bent low and I followed her as quietly as I could. Moccasins make little noise unless one steps on a twig or dislodges a stone. We stopped behind a boulder and looked down upon the little plain we had crossed. It was almost as light as day, and we could see the men plainly. But there was nothing in the arroyo — nothing.

"Where are they?" I murmured.

"They did not try to cross, or we would have heard. Now nobody could possibly make it."

The light of a big fire was reflected by the lake. There were no more shots near it, but an occasional one from various directions told us the cavalry was still finding and killing ours.

"Victorio?" I asked.

"All are dead."

"Grandfather?"

"He might have had a chance to escape. He would know it was too late to help those at the lake, and his duty is to live and save the helpless. Nana lives. So do your uncles. They will not leave us."

"Grandmother? Siki?"

She shook her head.

"Chenleh?"

She began to cry softly but stifled her sobs.

"Why did they build the big fire?"

"If they are taking prisoners they drag them near the fire and tie them. If not — they burn the bodies."

All the rest of that night we struggled in an ascent, stumbling, falling, scrambling over ledges, but making steady progress over the ridges. Toward morning, when we could go no further, we rested in a thicket until we got so cold we had to move. We had not eaten for twenty-four hours; we had no food, for the emergency bag had been tied to the mule. So had the blankets. Mother had a knife — nothing but a knife. But with a knife, an Apache can survive.

When light began to show we were well across the ridges. I trudged beside Mother, stopping when she did, dropping to the ground when she did. We stopped to breathe and I fell asleep; when I waked she was carrying me. I asked her to let me walk and she did. We heard the thud of moccasins and saw a man coming, staggering as he walked. His left arm dangled with blood dripping from it. Mother ran to him. She did not know him, but he was Apache. She cut and peeled long shoots and tore up his shirt to bind them to his arm. He was so weak he could hardly stand.

"How did you escape?"

"I was returning from the hunting trip. I rode in just as the attack began. A bullet struck me from my horse. They must have thought I was dead. They took my rifle and ammunition belt. When I regained consciousness I lay still till I felt sure no one was near. Then I crawled away."

"What are we to do?"

"Get to Nana. If we go west and cross a narrow plain we will find him in a deep arroyo — one deep enough to hide horses. It will soon be too light to risk it. Take your boy and go. I am too weak."

She pulled his arm across her shoulder and started to walk slowly. I stumbled across a vine and found some green gourds. I tried to eat one.

"Chew the pulp but do not swallow it," cautioned Mother.

It was very bitter, but there was a little juice in it.

"Someone's coming," said the man.

We stood motionless. We saw a young woman coming toward us with a water jug. She, too, was strange, but she was an Apache. She gave us water and mesquite-bean meal. Then she helped Mother with the wounded man. She pointed out the hiding place in which we would find Grandfather and returned to find and aid more refugees. We stayed in hiding until dark.[1]

The Survivors

Mangus, son of Mangas Coloradas, was standing guard. He took us to Nana. They had food and water, but little ammunition. Two men were with them, both wounded, but not badly. There were several women and children, and shortly after we arrived three more women came. In all, there were seventeen survivors. This number did not, of course, include the hunting party that had gone out before the attack, nor the warriors on the ammunition raid. It was doubtful, Grandfather said, that either group would find us soon.

Mother cut some leaves from a bunch of *nopal* and rubbed the thorns from it with a stick, for Nana dared not risk building a fire. She split the leaves and bound the fleshy side to the men's wounds. Nana helped her as gently and skillfully as Lozen could have.

When they had finished Nana talked to us. The chief had died as he would have wished — in the defense of his people. He was the greatest of all Apache chiefs, yes, of all Indian chiefs. He had died as he had lived, free and unconquerable. We knew well the fate of Mangas Coloradas and of Cochise. They, too, would have preferred death in battle; they would have envied Victorio. So — we were not to mourn for him. He had been spared the ignominy of imprisonment and slavery, and for that he would have been thankful to Ussen. His courage was to be the inspiration of those left to carry on our race, and fortunately there were enough women and warriors that our people might increase.

It was for us to rally and carry on the struggle.

There was a prolonged silence, broken by my mother.

"My mother?" she asked.

"I do not know whether or not my sister lives," replied Nana. "You say she followed Loco's daughter [Siki] to protect her. It is likely that the Mexicans have spared the young woman for slavery. But it is their custom to kill the old. I am afraid that your mother has ridden the Ghost Pony. That she would prefer to slavery."

"Did you find the bodies?"

"Our first obligation is to the living. Suldeen and Blanco are searching for the wounded and helpless. The Mexicans fight bravely against the unarmed."

"Blanco's wife?" asked Mother.

There was no answer.

"Your baby?" Nana asked Mother.

She pulled her blanket over her head. I knew that if Eclode lived my sister did. We were never to know what became of her.

That night Blanco and Kaytennae came in with ammunition, much ammunition.

"Too late," said Kaytennae, bitterly.

Grandfather spoke proudly, "It is not too late so long as one Apache lives. You have done well, my sons. You are tired and hungry. When you have eaten you must be in readiness to follow the Mexican cavalry, for it is possible that you can rescue prisoners. I will lead you."

"When we have eaten we start," answered Kaytennae, "but we need fresh horses. Ours are ridden down."

"I have horses. But first you must sleep. I will stand guard till you've had some rest. I was too hasty. Nothing can be accomplished by men exhausted as you are.

"The large party of soldiers headed for Chihuahua with about a hundred captives. You are too few to attack them. A smaller group went north. How many of our people they took I do not know. They followed a circuitous trail which I know well. I know also a short cut that should enable us to save much time and reach an ambush through which they will pass. We will wait there for them."

There were more of the cavalry than Nana had anticipated. His men lay hidden until all had passed. They had only one captive, a young girl. She rode behind a soldier. Kaytennae whistled the quail call, very softly. She raised her head. At the second signal she slipped off the horse and ran back toward the rocks. Kaytennae fired and the soldier fell. The cavalry fled, but Kaytennae had not enough men to pursue. No Apache was expendable.

They brought Dah de glash to Mother. She could tell us very little. She and her mother had unsaddled when the first shots warned them of ambush. They ran toward the mountain until a bullet struck her mother and killed her. The girl made sure she was dead before continuing her flight. Soldiers cut off her escape. They dragged her to the big fire and tied her to a mesquite bush with her back to the blaze. They brought in many other captives and bound them. There might have been a hundred in all — she did not know how many. Women and children, no men. Some young boys — half-grown. She smelled burning flesh . . . . .

The chief? She did not know.

She had not been molested. Before dawn the soldiers had forced her to mount behind one, and had ridden away. We knew the rest.

Nana sent men to the lake to bury our dead. They were cautious, for the Mexicans knew our custom and might lie in hiding to ambush the burial party. They did not go to the lake until the third day. Many bodies had been burned.

"Victorio?"

"We found the chief with his own knife in his heart. His ammunition belt was empty. Behind rocks we found three of his men who had died by their own knives, as had Victorio. The others had been killed by Mexicans. Those men we buried. We placed them beside big boulders and covered them with stones as best we could. We had nothing with which to dig.

"And the others — most of them partially burned — we could do nothing but cover. The living need us worse than our brave dead. We began a search for any who might be in hiding or wounded."

"Enjuh!" said Grandfather.

"Now it is for the living to see that our tribe is not exterminated. We must live. We must carry on the fight. Our wounded are weak, but are able to ride. At moonrise we start. Sleep until I call."

That terrible night ride! With the hoofs of the horses muffled by buckskin covering, we rode until almost dawn. I think there could not have been a more unhappy, hopeless people than we. Mounted behind Mother I sobbed, and I knew that she did. There was not one but that had lost members of his family, if not all of them. No warrior knew whether his wife lay dead or was a slave in the hands of the Mexicans. No one but Nana seemed to care whether he lived or died. But before daylight with Grandfather we lay hidden, for he knew every trail, every water hole, every cache. He knew how to evade the cavalry scouring the plains for us. He knew where other refugees might be found if any survived. Here and there he recruited a man for our little band. He sent men to Ojo Caliente and the Black Range to summon those who had been left in hiding because they were wounded. Gradually, one man at a time, he increased his force, though in comparison with Victorio's it was but a handful.

Believing that the Mexicans would expect him to go to Casas Grandes he bore to the north and approached the border south of the Floridas. To avoid pursuit he picked up only the horses needed for food. He knew every edible plant and animal. He sternly forbade taking horses until his men could take an entire *remuda*. They eagerly sought the opportunity. When it came, Mother and four other women rode with the warriors. They swooped down upon two *vaqueros* moving a herd of horses, shot them, waved their blankets and stampeded the *remuda* into a little canyon. They stretched ropes across the entrance and roped out fresh mounts. Our jaded ones followed, and they drove the rest before them.

As we approached the border, warning flashes told Nana that cavalry was moving. We took cover in a little side canyon and lay hidden while Blue Coats rode into Mexico. The United States was sending cavalry below the line to join those of Chihuahua in running us down. I think we did not stay there but a few hours, but in that time Mother got calico and muslin from a cache and supplied the men with new breech clouts. She had no time for dresses, but took enough material to replenish our clothing.

As we rode out, we met Sánchez and others of the hunting party. They had returned to Tres Castillos, and had followed us. They had followed the trail of the main force of cavalry long enough to know that they had about a hundred prisoners, and had taken them to Chihuahua, the City of Mules. With this additional force, Nana gave the Blue Coats and the Mexicans the slip by circling to the west and entering the United States near the Arizona line. Though it was cold in the Mogollons, game was plentiful, as were water and wood. Again we hid for several weeks while the caches were restocked with meat and other foods. The women made dresses, harvested and prepared food, and replenished the supply of moccasins.

Mother and two other women wandered far from camp. I was with them, and we saw that we could not get back before dark. We knew that we had to cross the stream on the fallen log by which we had come, but had difficulty in finding it. The women got ahead of us and we could not keep up. We did not know whether the log was up or down stream. We heard two shots, and lay hidden till we got so cold we had to move. Seldom did one of our race get lost, but we had done so. We worked up stream, as the women had done, but found neither them nor the log. Then we turned back and stumbled along in the dark, hunting the crossing. When light came we recognized no landmarks. I think it must have been noon before we found the foot log. When we reached camp the others had come in, but all thought we had been shot, or killed by grizzly bears or mountain lions, numerous in that area.

After that experience Nana told me stories of Child of the Waters. He had been required to overcome difficulties. His life had been a series of them. Grandfather impressed upon me that every struggle, whether won or lost, strengthens us for the next to come. It is not good for people to have an easy life. They become weak and inefficient when they cease to struggle. Some need a series of defeats before developing the strength and courage to win a victory.

Child of the Waters had overcome many enemies, Giant Buffalo, Giant Bear, Giant Deer, and Giant Owl; there was one other which we do not name. All these were enemies of our people who hunted down and killed them. The Apaches especially feared this Nameless Creature, which though resembling man, was not human. It had Power — great Power with its eyes. Nobody could look at this Thing and live. Fortunately it could not see well at a distance, otherwise the Apaches would have been exterminated.

There was also a creature who was a friend to Child of the Waters. It crept upon four legs and He called it Giant Lizard. Child of the Waters had thought this Nameless Monster to be the only one of its kind, but Giant Lizard told Him that at the top of a mountain, in a crater, the Nameless Monster had hidden a loathsome family. All were immense, but not so large as the *Yehyeh*. All possessed the Power to kill by looking at one.

Child of the Waters was still a child, but He had killed the terrible *Yehyeh* and He set Himself the impossible task of destroying these monsters. For it was the mission of Child of the Waters to preserve mankind. He asked the advice of His friend, Giant Lizard.

"The Things up there see me about and do not fear me," said Lizard. "They think me harmless. Get under my belly, hold on to me, and I will carry you to the crater. In that hole there is always fire. The walls are blackened by it. They are steep and so straight that only the Great One can get out of them. Take this buckskin bag with you; when I reach the top and can look over into the pit, use it."

Child of the Waters obeyed, and, as the Lizard has said, the Things paid no attention to him. The Child peered over the edge and saw the Things about the flames. He emptied the bag of powder into the fire, and terrible fumes arose. The Things were blinded, and he killed them with his arrows. Last, he killed the Great One.

These things Child of the Waters did before He joined Ussen in the Happy Land.

In our tongue the Child is called *Too bah ghees chin en*. It was His teachings that Blanco stressed, especially when he told us time after time that we are to show mercy to any enemy who throws down his weapons and surrenders. Such an enemy is not to be killed, and he is not to be mistreated if he is kept as a captive and is loyal to the tribe. Nana's Mexican boys were still with us, and I knew they were accepted and treated as well as our own. I thought, though, of the mass murder of my people at Tres Castillos when the warriors were away. I wondered if the Mexicans were as kind to the prisoners as we are to our captives.

We were near Horse Springs in a country of ranches [Western New Mexico]. White Eyes had herds of cattle roaming over the land, and they sometimes sent children out to drive them. One evening Kaytennae came in with two of these, a boy not much older than I, and a girl almost grown. Both were riding one horse. Nana looked at the frightened things with disgust.

"These are puny things, unfit for life. The boy is already too old to be trained for war. The girl would be a constant handicap to us. The ranchers will search for them — are probably already on our trail. Soon they will notify the cavalry."

Kaytennae bowed his head.

"You brought them. Dispose of them."

Mother took them to our shelter that night and fed them.

The next morning Kaytennae led their horse to the back of the line, for he was on rear guard. When we stopped for the night they did not appear.

"Where are they?" demanded Nana.

"They escaped," solemnly replied Kaytennae.

Grandfather chuckled.

"What happened?" I asked.

"He turned them loose," said Mother. "If they are intelligent they'll give the horse his head and he'll take them home."

•   •   •

One day Mother told me a secret, and warned me that it was not to be repeated. I was very happy.

"Does Kaytennae know?" I asked.

"Kaytennae, Grandfather, and Blanco know."

"Then it may be mentioned to them?"

She nodded. I asked Kaytennae when he was to be my father.

"Would you like that?"

"More than anything in the world."

There was much hunting and preparation of food. In a secluded spot my people prepared the wedding feast, and for four days and nights they sang and danced. At the fire the first evening I asked, "Are you my father now?"

"Not until the end of the fourth day, Little Son."

"It seems queer that it takes four days to become a father."

He laughed, but I did not mind that for I knew Kaytennae loved me. I told him so, and also that I hoped he would love Mother. He promised that he would, and again he laughed.

Among other foods my people had baked the heads of cattle in pits, and they were taken out the evening of the fourth day. Though there was much good meat nothing was so tempting as that tender delicious part on the heads. People took their portions and sat about eating, paying no attention to me. I slipped near the food, got myself a generous serving from a head, and hid to eat it. It was so good that I helped myself to a second portion. When I had eaten it I stretched out in the bushes to wait for what was to come. I had no doubt whatever but that I would die. I had never seen anything die a natural death, though I knew it happened. Everything died by violence, and I wondered if I would suffer. It was queer that I felt no pain . . . . .

I was awakened by Nana's singing The Morning Song, and found myself in his arbor, wrapped in his blanket.[1]

My Uncles

Regardless of where an atrocity was committed it was attributed to Nana. When these events occurred simultaneously in different areas, Nana had divided his forces, but was responsible. Some of these reports were true, some not. Reports of his killings were exaggerated as were those of Victorio's. No living person knows better than I that both exacted lives in retaliation for those of my people who were killed, but not many know the provocation they had for revenge.

Thomas Cruse, later a brigadier general, was a lieutenant at the time of the Victorio campaign. In *Apache Days and After,* he wrote "The Government ignored Victorio's just grievances and forced him to the warpath. The ultimate cost was millions in money and over a thousand lives of white men, women and children." Gatewood, who knew the circumstances, always said that any man of discretion, empowered to adjust Victorio's well-founded claims, could have prevented the bloody and disastrous outbreak of 1879.

That statement I believe true. Unfortunately, the few who possessed the knowledge had not the power to act. Nana, deeply and sincerely wanted peace, but he wanted his own country, his freedom, and that of his people to enjoy living in their own land. Aged and infirm, he fought for people, land, and freedom to the inevitable, tragic end. If he were ill or weary, only he knew it. His endurance seemed endless, his patience effortless. No young man in the tribe could spend more hours in the saddle without rest than he. I am sure Mother realized that he was often weary and discouraged, but she did not speak of it in my presence. He continued to set the pace for the young men, always taking upon himself whatever hazards had to be met. If he depended upon anyone it was Kaytennae.

After we turned south, Nana took half the warriors with him and put Blanco in command of the others who were to take the non-combatants to Sonora. Two of the women who accompanied him were highly skilled in dressing wounds, and while not as expert as Lozen, were efficient fighters. These were exempt from cooking and other chores usually done by the wives who accompanied their husbands, or the young boys in training as warriors.

Our group went by Ojo Caliente, deserted by the soldiers. Blanco stationed guards to warn us of the approach of an enemy and for two days we stayed near the warm spring. How good it was to lie in that water! If we had been able to bathe it had been in cold mountain streams. On the desert where even drinking water was difficult to obtain we had rubbed our skins with fine sand. We lay in the cleansing pool and enjoyed its beneficent water for hours.

We left by Monticello and turned south toward Fort Cumimngs. We were to go west through Cook's Pass. Nana made a feint at attack to lure the cavalry toward the Floridas so that Blanco could take the emigrant wagon road west from the fort. The plan worked out as Grandfather had intended. He rode close enough to Fort Cummings to be sighted; then dashed toward the Floridas with the cavalry in pursuit. He knew that not all the soldiers would leave the fort, but that the one white officer and the few Negroes would not be very formidable.

When the dust cloud had faded in the south Blanco rode boldly to the spring under the very walls of the fort and watered his horses. Then we took the road west through the canyon at the foot of Standing Mountain [Cook's Peak] which had long been used by us for a lookout. Dah de glash and some boys drove the *remuda*. Blanco scouted ahead. The women and small children came next; then the rest of the men, with Kaytennae, constituting the rear guard. When we were more than halfway through, Blanco signaled for Kaytennae to join him, and sent him ahead to scout the fort beyond the west end of the pass.

Blanco gave orders that we were not to follow him closely but to keep within sight and watch for signals. He had little concern for attack from the rear, for he had taken care of that. Ahead lay uncertainty. At bends in the canyon he waited until we came in sight. The trip was uneventful until nearly completed. Then we saw Blanco on a little hill, facing us. He signaled for us to hurry. Suddenly he raised his rifle high. That meant we were being pursued. We put the horses to the run and pulled up when we reached the hill.

"Dust behind you!" he shouted. "Cavalry! Dismount and take cover."

Both horses and people were well concealed before the cavalry came in sight. Whether or not it was from Fort Cummings we never knew. The men rode not as though in pursuit of an enemy, but in a leisurely manner taking no precautions against being ambushed. Blanco let them ride to the spring and dismount. At his signal the men fired at the horses. Despite their negligence in reading sign, those Negro soldiers acquitted themselves well. They used the fallen horses for cover and put up a good defense until the white officer ordered a retreat. He may have been inexperienced. He was certainly frightened. As they fled back over the road to Fort Cummings our men followed and killed more. Fearing that it might be a ruse to draw us into ambush Blanco did not follow far.

Suddenly two Negro cavalrymen dashed on foot into the mouth of a dry arroyo and disappeared around a bend. Blanco ran after them. Suldeen called to him to stop but he went on. Mother had mounted with me behind her; she followed my uncle, and we got a glimpse of him as he ran around a bend. We heard two shots. Kaytennae and Suldeen rode past us calling to Mother to go back. We saw them dismount to cross some debris, and then they went out of sight. Mother and I got off her horse and followed. We saw Blanco lying in the sand. Kaytennae and Suldeen had gone on after the Negroes. As we bent over the body we heard more shots.

Under an overhanging bank Kaytennae and Suldeen scooped a hole in the sand. They placed Blanco's body in it, laid his rifle by him, and covered him with Mother's blanket. They piled rocks over the grave and collapsed the bank upon it. Then we returned to the rest.

Suldeen bade them not grieve for his brother who was no longer a hunted thing, fleeing from his own land, but happy in the Place of the Dead. Ussen had spoken to Blanco, even as He had to Victorio. Each knew his time was near, and each met it fearlessly. It was not they who were unfortunate, but we who had been driven like animals from our own homes, and who had nothing ahead but slavery or death. The bad thing was the loss of a warrior to defend the helpless. Let every man remember that not one could be spared and take precautions to live for the defense of his people.

Then Suldeen rode ahead in his brother's place. Kaytennae scouted before him and brought word that the west end of Cook's Pass was guarded and that we must seek an exit to the south. Suldeen rode to the crest of a ridge and signalled for the rest to follow. The mountain to the north was too steep for even an Apache to climb, and southward was our only way of escape. Suldeen rode through timber and rounded a turn. Then he came back. There were three tents barring our passage. Not ranchers nor cowboys — miners. Cavalry might be closing in from either end of the pass, and he could do nothing but attack. Mangus and my young uncle were to circle far to the west with the women and children, and the men to ride straight for the tents. The survivors were to head for the border and ride fast.

"If we live, Kaytennae and I will overtake you."

Mother caught her breath. Then she said, "You heard; Ussen has spoken, and Suldeen is to die."

"Do not let them attack," I begged.

She shook her head and pulled aside as the noncombatants left. The two men rode hard toward the tents. There was a shot and Suldeen fell from his horse. Kaytennae leaped to the ground and dropped into an arroyo. Mother followed, with me behind her. Before we could overtake Kaytennae, she had her rifle in readiness. We heard two shots and knew that he had accounted for two men. As we passed the mouth of a side arroyo I saw the shadow of a rifle move. *"Indah!"* I shouted.[1] Kaytennae was racing toward us, but it was Mother who got the first shot. There was no need for another.

They scouted the terrain carefully before burying Suldeen. Then we saw no more enemies, and we followed our people. Mangus had sent Dah de glash and the small boys ahead to scout. Late at night Kaytennae selected a place to stop.

He anticipated pursuit and hid the horses a long distance from our camp. At dawn we started south. It was not long before a dust cloud in the east moved parallel with us. When we went down the west side of a ridge we hoped to lose it, but upon emerging upon the plain saw that it was coming toward us. From the hilltop Kaytennae identified the riders as Nana's band. Soon Nana joined us. What a difference Grandfather's presence made! Led by that frail, aged man, ours was again a fighting unit with renewed hope and courage. What though the Blue Coats followed us and the Mexican cavalry lay in waiting for us to cross the border? Grandfather had proved himself invincible against unsurmountable obstacles and impossible odds.

He knew of caches where food and ammunition were stored. He knew where horses could be concealed. I never knew of his abandoning nor killing the horses. It may have been because of his lameness that he did not, but I think that it was his intelligence that enabled him to preserve his mounts where other leaders would have slain them. People on foot have a much greater chance of concealment than mounted ones.

As we moved to the border more dust was sighted, this time ahead. It was not the compact cloud raised by cavalry, but the long thin cloud, from riders in single file. Either Apaches or a mule train! Ammunition, perhaps! Nana went into ambush with warriors on either side of the canyon through which the coming riders must pass.

We were upon one of the many smugglers' trails which crossed the border at intervals. From behind a rock high on one side of the narrow canyon Mother and I saw the first movement of the oncoming travelers. Mules! It was a mule train laden with great bags of heavy stuff — ammunition, perhaps. Men walked beside the pack animals, apparently not expecting attack.[2] They were taken by surprise and made little defense. Grandfather did not wait to inspect the booty but turned the train about and crossed into Mexico. Not until evening did he stop. There, in an arroyo fringed by cottonwoods he planned to fill the ammunition belts and cache what he could not take with him. Two heavy leather bags were lugged from a mule. I will never forget the disgust on his face when he ripped one open. He drew a heavy dull bar from it and let it drop to the ground.

"Silver!" he snorted, contemptuously.

"No ammunition!" said Sánchez.

"After all the waste of time, life, and bullets! This worthless stuff!"

"We have the mules, and the ammunition in the belts —"

Sánchez lifted the bar. It was about as long as my arm and thick as a man's. And men had died for this stuff! He spoke to Nana, "If we could get this to Casas Grandes we could trade it to the Mexicans for things of value to us. It is too heavy to move unless we trudge beside the mules. We might be attacked and forced to leave it. But if each man took two or three bars to trade for bullets —"

"Instead of ammunition he would get mescal and be killed."

Sánchez dropped the bar. He knew well that Nana feared his craving for liquor.

"Then why not bury it?" asked Sánchez, "We might come back for it some time."

Nana assented and a long shallow hole was scooped in the sandy bed of the arroyo. When the metal had been covered, stones and driftwood were thrown over the sand so that it looked undisturbed. A bar had been overlooked. Nana did not wish to wait for it to be buried with the rest and had Kaytennae place it in the fork of a cottonwood as a marker. It seemed to me that my stepfather obeyed reluctantly; and I saw that he was looking about carefully as though he wished to be able to recognize the place again. Nana missed nothing. He told Kaytennae that evening by the fire that he knew of several places where either gold or silver was to be found in abundance. "There is a canyon in the mountains west of Ojo Caliente — a long way west — where chunks of the yellow stuff as large as grains of corn can be picked up if I did not fear the wrath of Ussen. I know of cliffs with layers of silver so soft that it can be cut with a knife. I know a cave where bars of gold are stacked as is firewood by the soldiers."

Kaytennae asked no questions but his eyes glittered. Never before had Nana mentioned ore to us. We listened eagerly. "Just beneath the rim of a cliff I found a cave almost filled with it. It could not be reached from above, so the Mexicans must have carried those bars up ladders from one ledge to another to hide it."

"Where?" breathed Kaytennae.

"In Juh's country, a three-day walk from Casas Grandes. But remember this: No man disobeys the commands of Ussen without punishment. With Perico and Martine, I climbed to that place once, but we did not touch the accursed stuff."

"But it will buy ammunition."

"Why buy what we can take?"

Grandfather led us to the deep *barrancas* on the west slope of the Sierra Madre. The walls are precipitous, but my people found places where they could be scaled. He took us to a sort of plateau upon the north side of one, with a path to the water's edge. This level plot was several acres in extent, and wooded. The approach to it was a winding path, very narrow, one that a few men could easily defend against many. In that place we lived a few weeks as those who have gone to the Happy Place must. Again we hunted, feasted, and danced about fires. Again fathers spent time with their families — those who had fathers left to them. Food supplies were prepared, supplies of clothing replenished. The little remnant of Victorio's people enjoyed the security and abundance so long promised, so long sought. For the first time within my memory we lived as Apaches had before the coming of White Eyes.

Kaytennae was a kind father. He was not indulgent, for he trained me for survival, and that does not admit of softness. Nana had brought Istee, a handsome and intelligent lad about three years older than I, and the son of Victorio. He had also brought the wife and son of Mangus.[3] They had not accompanied us to Mexico, but had been hidden in the Black Range.

The little girls in the band received the same training as the boys. Each day all practiced with bow and arrows, sling and spears. Each was taught to mount an unsaddled horse without help. We caught the mane, dug our toes into the foreleg, and swung ourselves astride the animal. Then we had to become able to leap astride the horse without a handhold. That was difficult, but we learned by running down a slope for the takeoff. At first we threw ourselves face down across the back of the Spanish pony, and wriggled into a sitting position. I think it may have been three months before I could perform the feat on level ground.

From the canyon the men made raids on villages, but not those close to us. Once Kaytennae returned with three Mexican boys, one of whom he gave to Nana to serve as his orderly. The others lived with us. In a sense they were slaves, but they were treated as well as I. One was half-grown, a handsome lad, and a very apt pupil. Kaytennae planned to make a warrior of him. The other was less capable, but obedient and courteous. Soon the older was given the name — He Who Steals Love — because of his personality. The other was called Boy. All children were under rigid discipline but it did not include physical punishment. They were eager for the approval of the older people, and strove for it.

The captives acquired our language readily, although it is not an easy tongue to learn. They, like our own lads, took care of the horses and performed other necessary tasks about camp. These found it humiliating, just as I did, to be surpassed by the girls, and worked hard to excel.

Neither a chief nor his children had any special privileges. Both Istee and Frank Mangus did as much work as the captives. Only my being younger was a barrier to my efforts. The captive boys were skillful with horses, and with us took care of them. They were permitted to go on raids for acquiring them, a privilege I was too young to share. Not once did either attempt to escape. My young uncle always rode with Kaytennae on these raids.

He had been very quiet since the death of his elder brothers. The men knew he was depressed and understood the cause, but it was not our custom to extend sympathy in words. Instead we sought to stimulate his pride by taking him on raids. Nothing succeeded in arousing him to the normal attitude of a young warrior.

Nana suggested a change of tactics, that of sending him on a mission where he would be forced to fight. Mother asked Kaytennae to look out for her brother and he reminded her that the suggestion was an insult to a warrior. This young man had been trained to fight, and to protect himself, not to require the services of a grandmother. She knew that Kaytennae was right, and said nothing more.

They returned without him. They had encountered a troop of Mexican cavalry but discovered their nearness in time to take cover. The young man gave a very good account of himself during the fight and the warriors thought their ruse had been successful. Without their knowledge he rode alone in pursuit of the cavalry. They found and buried his body.

$\mathcal{L}$*ozen*

He Who Steals Love reported to Grandfather that a rider was coming, a rider leading a pack horse. He thought it was a woman.

"Coming openly?"

"Yes, and stopping to read sign. She has a rifle."

Nana sat very still. Then he ordered his horse and rode to meet her. He knew before he saw her that it was Lozen who came, Lozen, who had dropped from the line to care for the young mother. She was well armed, well mounted, and well equipped. She had taken her charges to their people at the Mescalero Reservation and followed us to the Black Range, and then to Mexico. She had ridden alone through enemy territory, and evaded the cavalry of both the United States and Mexico.

I had heard much of her as a warrior, but had not seen her in action. She must have been at least forty years old but was as agile as any man among us. In her youth she could outrun any of the men, but she no longer competed in races. In other athletic feats she was remarkable, but the men did not resent her. They were frankly proud of her and her ability. Above all they respected her integrity.

Lozen spoke nothing of her experiences until Nana questioned her, and then she did so reluctantly. She had hoped to get the Mescalero woman some distance off the trail, but the cavalry came so soon they were compelled to hide, scarcely a stone's throw away.

[115]

Fortunately the soldiers were riding hard and paying little attention to anything but those they were pursuing. It was their return trip that Lozen feared, for they might take time to do some scouting. While they rode to the river she got the helpless girl to a secluded place and attended her during the birth of her baby. Evidently the soldiers did not discover that any had been left, and made no effort to find them.

Lozen had her rifle, cartridge belt, and a knife. The girl had kept her blanket. They wrapped the child in a piece torn from it and Lozen left her to find a better hiding place. Under an overhanging rock they took shelter. The next day they made their way to the river, and camped. Lozen had a supply of food for about three days. There were Mexicans across the Río Grande, and she could not risk firing a shot. She hid by the stream beside a path upon which cattle had come to drink. Killing a longhorn with a knife is a feat that few men would undertake, but Lozen did it. She cut strips of the meat and carried it to their retreat. They sliced and dried it.

Neither had a water jug, and it was hazardous to attempt to travel without one. It was a long distance between water holes, and they could not risk walking. She decided to cross the river and get a horse. We had forded it, but rains in the mountains had caused the Río Grande to flood. She decided that she could swim it. Before making the attempt she instructed the young mother as to her procedure in case Lozen did not return. The girl could not travel without a cradle. They made a crude one. Lozen cut willow shoots and bent one for the frame. The blanket served as a cover for it. She gave the girl careful directions, and left all her equipment except her knife.

From the hide she cut a long strip to serve as a bridle, and with it tied to her belt, and her knife in its sheath, she watched till night fell. Mexican women came to the stream to fill their *ollas*. These were made of clay and had been fired, but they would break easily. Nevertheless, with one of those the journey would be much safer. Stealing one from the village would be dangerous because of the vicious dogs.

Then, unexpectedly, Mexican cavalry rode down to water their horses. Undoubtedly they would camp for the night, perhaps for several nights, but she could not depend upon that. She must obtain a horse before morning. She watched the soldiers make camp about a half-mile up the stream. It might be possible to procure a horse from them without arousing the dogs. She moved opposite them and studied the surroundings. Banks were steep but not impassable; she would make the attempt there.

After they went to sleep she swam across and hid to watch.

The men, wrapped in *serapes,* lay about the fire. The horses were hobbled a short distance from them, and a guard paced back and forth between the two groups. She could see him pass the dying fire as he plodded in front of it. She studied the horses. They seemed a bit restless — probably smelled her. So long as they didn't snort nor attempt to break from their hobbles the guard might not detect her presence. She knew that she could not hope to get a saddle, for the men slept with their heads on them. Nor would she have time for that.

When the guard left the horses and started toward the fire she must make her attempt to secure one. Already she had selected a powerful steed, one of the most restless. When the guard had passed the fire she would tie her leather rope around its lower jaw, cut the hobbles and ride. She crept softly to the animal, and quickly tied the rope. When she bent to cut the hobbles it snorted and plunged. She leaped to its back and turned it toward the river. Bullets whizzed past her head as the horse slid down the bank and plunged into the water. It was scrambling up the opposite bank before men could follow. A few bullets were fired across the river, but she was soon out of range.

Before daylight the women had covered many miles. Much of the time Lozen walked, but toward morning she mounted in front of the girl, for she wished to reach a hiding place before dawn. She found one on the south side of a ridge, with a water hole beyond. They camped under an overhanging bank, well screened by vegetation. They had food but no water; they chewed the pulp of the *nopal,* grateful for the small amount of moisture. Lozen climbed to the crest of the ridge and found that the cavalry was camped about the water hole she had hoped to reach. Those who had chased Victorio into Mexico had received reenforcements. That meant they would attempt to prevent the return of the Indians. It meant, too, that there were undoubtedly guards at all the water holes, and that it would be extremely difficult, with her encumbrances, to cross to the next chain of mountains.

She saw a deer but dared not risk a shot. There was little probability of cattle coming near, for the place was very barren. She had a supply of dried beef which she had hoped to save for emergencies, but had to eat part of it during the three days they stayed. During that time they improved the makeshift cradle. They resoled their moccasins, and they reconnoitered.

They needed water so desperately that Lozen returned to the river. She decided to cross into Mexico, detour to the west, and reenter the United States. The cavalry had gone and she decided to cross near their camp. The horse could not carry all at one trip, so she took the baby across first and hung the cradle from a limb while she returned for the mother. With the girl astride it the horse towed Lozen. Had she been alone she would not have hesitated to swoop past a *chosa* (Mexican hut) and grab an *olla* from the *vigas* (roof beams), but she did not wish to jeopardize the lives of her charges. A saddle, too, would have to be given up until there was a better opportunity of securing one.

She set out southwest and did not stop until coming light made it dangerous for them to ride. The land was sparsely settled, the big haciendas being of vast extent, and the casas miles apart. Clustered about the huge houses of the *ricos* were the *chosas* of the *peons,* the church, the corrals, and the storehouses. The headquarters was in reality a village, protected both by dogs and guards. She hoped to find a line camp with not more than two *vaqueros.* From such a place she might be able to get a saddle, and possibly another horse.

It was weeks before she found what she sought. Meanwhile she killed a calf, dried the meat, and made a leather bag for the *tunas,* fruit of the *nopal,* which they gathered.

Water was the most difficult problem. She used the stomach of the calf for a container, but it did not hold enough to supply their needs.

After weeks she followed three *vaqueros* to their isolated camp. One dismounted to pull thorn brush from an opening in a corral, an opening so narrow that only one horse at a time could pass. In one corner of the corral was an adobe shed with a low thatched roof. It opened inside, with a door so low that the horses' backs brushed it as they entered.

The men slept outside, wrapped in serapes. Each evening they penned enough horses to catch the ones they wanted from the *remuda*. In the morning they pulled the thorny brush from the gate so that they could pass, single file. From a box on the roof they took nubbins of blue corn for the horses they saddled. They had no dogs.

Lozen waited for the dark of the moon. In the evening she stationed woman, baby, and food bag in a shallow arroyo with the horse. At dawn the girl was to mount and wait under a tree that would serve Lozen as a landmark. When the *vaquero* who dragged the brush away for the horses had cleared the opening, a horse shot from the shed with a slender figure lying flat upon it. Before they could saddle and give chase Lozen had picked up her charges and they were off.

She needed still another saddle, but an inquisitive cavalryman supplied that. He also furnished another rifle, ammunition, a blanket and a shirt. Most prized of all his equipment was a canteen. Well stocked for both traveling and defense, Lozen set out for Mescalero and delivered her dependents to their people.

From them she learned of the Massacre of Tres Castillos and the death of her brother. Some of the Mescaleros who had gone off with Victorio had been killed, but the majority had returned to their people, and among them Eclode.

"What of my baby?" Mother asked.

"I did not know of her loss, so I did not ask."

Knowing that few of her people were alive Lozen felt that they needed her, and she set out to find them. Freed of her encumbrances she made good time while following our route. Nobody needed tell her to be cautious, for she was resourceful and cunning. She knew well that when she found us the danger would be great, but she wished to help her people, and she did. She was with Geronimo on his last outbreak. She went to Florida with us, and to Alabama. When I returned from Carlisle to Mother and Kaytennae, I inquired about her. She had died in Alabama.[1]

During this interval after Victorio was buried Nana took revenge for the murder of his people. I do not like to think of the things I witnessed. I have seen hundreds of people killed, but nobody tortured, nobody scalped. I believe that Nana was responsible for more deaths than either Geronimo or Victorio. But we did not have the mania for statistics that White Eyes do, and did not count the dead. Revenge was not forbidden to us; it was our obligation to retaliate for the wrongs inflicted upon us. Ussen had not commanded that we love our enemies. Nana did not love his; and he was not content with an eye for and eye, nor a life for a life. For every Apache killed he took many lives.

That was our custom — the custom of a primitive people who had been taught that revenge is obligatory. I am unable to see that these ethics differed materially from those of so-called civilized people. The difference lay mainly in the Apaches' honesty about what they were doing.

In the skirmishes and ambushes that occurred, Lozen fought with the warriors. Both Kaytennae and Grandfather praised her fighting qualities so highly that Mother was a bit resentful.

"I could do the same if I had anyone with whom to leave Kay-waykla," she told my stepfather.

"Fortunately you do not," replied Kaytennae. "I do not want you to risk your life in battle. I respect Lozen, but you are my wife."

Sonora

We kept close to the foothills as we worked our way south on the west side of the Blue Mountains. Many *barrancas* opened into them affording convenient concealment, with abundance of food available. Sonora was a much more productive land than Chihuahua. For a time we followed the course of a stream along which grew delicious fruit. We bathed in the river, and we saw that there were many fish in it, but we did not use them for food. To Apaches eating the flesh of fish or dog is repugnant.

Nana had traversed this trail previously and had an unerring memory for landmarks. He led us to a deserted village in a deep canyon. For the first time I saw palms and orange trees. For the first time I entered the dwelling of a White Eye. It was crumbling to ruin, and was dark and stuffy. I had the feeling of being in a trap. I wondered why the Mexicans preferred these dark, dismal houses to the fresh air and the stars, how they could rest in such a place. We did not spend the night there.

We reached a jungle with gorgeously colored birds and flowers. The steamy heat was oppressive and Nana went north, not retracing our route, but by another on which we harvested food. One night we made camp at the foot of a cliff; next morning Grandfather had the boys spread a skin on the ground. They began shooting arrows at a dark mass hanging from the ledge above. Chunks of it fell and broke;

Juh's Stronghold

ARIZONA

NEW MEXICO

DOUGLAS ●

● CANANEA

FRONTERAS ●

● BAVISPE

JANOS ●

JUH'S
STRONGHOLD

ARISPE ●

NACOZARI ●

CASAS
GRANDES ●

SIERRA MADRE
(BLUE MOUNTAINS)

HERMOSILLO ●

RIO SONORA

MEXICO

GULF
OF
CALIFORNIA

RIO YAQUI

something soft oozed from it. Grandfather picked up a piece and handed it to me. The other boys were eating it greedily. I tasted. It was delicious! I had never eaten anything so good. Mother squeezed pieces of comb with her hands and let the honey drip into a skin bag with a small mouth. So did many others. We took a great quantity of it. Except for baked mescal and dried fruit we had no sweets, and we liked them.

Toward the north end of the Blue Mountains we camped near a stream at the foot of a mile-high mountain. Nana rode to the entrance of a small canyon with a very narrow opening. He did not wait to scout it, but went straight to a camping place with smoke-blackened stones. He stationed Kaytennae and Sánchez outside the entrance, and sent He Who Steals Love to act as their messenger. When preparations had been made for the night Mother and I went to Kaytennae. He drank from the wicker jug. Then he pointed to the heights above us where a tiny fringe of green shimmered in the midday sun.

"Tall pines on the flat top of the mountain. Juh's stronghold. His lookout has seen us and men are coming down the Zigzag Trail. If you watch that white spot near the top you may see them cross it." Mother saw them before I did, but I was looking for horsemen, not a string of ants moving so slowly that it was hard to realize when they had disappeared against the dark wall.

This, then, was the Promised Land, the place where we were to find refuge. On top of that mountain we were to live in peace, with no more threats of attack, no more hiding, no more violent deaths. When Mother said so, Kaytennae shook his head.

"Not if I know Nana. He has recruited men; he has horses and ammunition. He has given his people a long rest and they have renewed strength and energy. As long as the chief lives he will fight.

"Go to Nana, *Gouyen,* and tell him that Juh comes. His men will be hungry. Prepare a feast for them."

It was sundown before the Nednhi reached the foot of the trail. Juh rode straight to our camping place and Nana met him there. He rode toward us, a powerful figure on a sturdy war horse much larger than the Spanish ponies we used. When he dismounted, He Who Steals Love took the reins. Others scrambled for those of the warriors as Juh embraced Grandfather. I think Nana must have been close to six feet in height, but Juh towered above him. He was very

Naiche, second son of the Chiricahua chief, Cochise. With Geronimo and others of his band, Naiche greeted the Warm Springs Apache who sought refuge at Juh's Stronghold in Sonora.

large, not fat, but stockily built. His body was twice as thick as Grandfather's. His heavy hair was braided and the ends fell almost to his knees. His features differed from those of the Warm Springs. They were what people now call Mongoloid. Perhaps it is true that our people crossed from Asia to Alaska centuries ago, though no Apache believes that they would have walked against the Sun. Always Indians of all tribes walked with it — never against it.

"When will we go up the trail?" I asked Mother.

She shook her head.

While we were feasting He Who Steals Love came to report that horsemen were crossing the river — Apaches. He had lain hidden until he saw the war paint on their faces.

"Why the war paint?" asked Grandfather.

"Geronimo," said Juh. "He likes to scare the Mexicans. He hates them with an intensity hardly believable. He rides prepared for battle. Let's play a joke on him."

Earth was thrown hastily over the fire and everybody sought cover along the walls of the winding canyon. Mother and I crouched behind a boulder with Kaytennae. In the twilight we could see them coming close. Geronimo rode ahead, taking no precautions against attack.

"He knows the Mexicans dare not come here," murmured Kaytennae.

The erect compact figure was smaller than that of Juh, but blocky and muscular. He rode in confidently, taking no precautions. Kaytennae let them pass. When Geronimo dismounted Grandfather arose.

"Welcome to my trap!" he called.

"I knew all the time you were here," was the reply.

"You did not," said Nana. "And you the sly fox of the Apaches!"

Grandfather greeted him with the *abrazo* of our people, and after him came a tall, stately, young man without paint.

"Naiche," murmured Mother, "son of the great Cochise."

Others crowded about them till I could no longer see the chiefs.

After they had eaten, the people made a great circle about the fire and the singers and drummers took their places. Our drums were a piece of hide stretched over a hoop, nothing more. The musicians faced the east and began singing while the warriors retired to the brush. Because we were in Juh's land the first call was for him. He came at the head of his warriors clad only in breech clout and moccasins, but they were gorgeously beaded. From the tight-fitting skull cap of the Nednhi Medicine Man floated long streamers of eagle plumes that dangled almost to his heels. He was followed by his men, whom Apaches consider the fiercest and most implacable of all our people. Last of all came Juh's son, Daklugie.

When they had danced four times around the circle, Juh stopped and began to sing. He had an impediment in his speech, but it did not affect his singing. He had a soft, deep voice and was skillful in improvising rhythmic accounts of the exploits of his band. When he had finished he and his men took their seats and a cry arose for Nana. My heart was thrilled by the ovation given him. He wore no finery such as Juh but had discarded his dingy shirt for the occasion. His body was emaciated, but he carried himself with such dignity that Juh was not more impressive. Fine clothing is not necessary to one who has the attributes of leadership. In spite of his stiff ankle he was dancing with grace and ease, equally as well as Kaytennae who followed him. After them came our men, not great in numbers, but famed for their fighting qualities.

"Why is not Sánchez next to Grandfather?" I asked.

"Nana has decided that Kaytennae is to be our next chief," proudly replied Mother. "I have hoped that this would be, but have not been sure before."

"And Mangus? He is the son of Mangas Coloradas."

She shook her head.

The four circles had been completed and our men were taking their seats. Cries went up for Geronimo. He responded, arrogantly.

I said so to Mother.

"All Apaches are arrogant," she replied. "They have a right to be."

"Not Grandfather," I protested.

"When it suits him to be. He is wise enough to conceal it, for above all, he knows the reaction of men, and he leads instead of driving his band."

Mother indicated Perico, half-brother to Geronimo. With her nose, as etiquette requires, she pointed out Fun and also Eyelash, half-brothers to Geronimo, and renowned for their prowess in battle. To many Apaches, Fun was the bravest of all the band, although none were lacking in courage. For the first time I saw Yanosha, another mighty warrior. He was followed by a small thin boy, little more than half-grown.

"His servant whom he is training to become a brave," explained Mother. "Kanseah. He is Geronimo's nephew."

"Will Nana train me?" I asked.

"Not unless you prove yourself worthy. The chief must choose the most worthy of the boys. It may not be a relative unless he has the approval of the warriors. See that you make yourself eligible."

"I don't see Naiche."

"Nor I. When Tahza was poisoned Naiche was too young to become the leader. He had not been trained for the place as had his brother because Cochise wanted his younger son to be loyal to Tahza. Both were very young when their father died, and Juh assumed the leadership. When the Chiricahua were robbed of their reservation and forced to go to San Carlos both Juh and Geronimo refused and fled to Mexico. They are brothers-in-law, and work well together. Juh married the favorite sister of Geronimo. She is a very shrewd and influential person, much like Lozen. She is not a warrior, but in other ways is powerful. It is thought that she suggests much of the strategy employed by them, but she is far too wise to admit it."

There was with Geronimo another Warm Springs leader who had a small band of his own. He was not affiliated with either Loco or Nana but operated independently. Though in later years he was known as Gordo (fat), as a young man he was very thin. He had brought no men with him, but perhaps because Geronimo wished to enlist his aid, he was recognized. Had the Apaches ever been able to effect a strong central organization, history might have been very different, but their weakness was that they could not combine their forces for any length of time.

I was still watching for Gordo to appear when something moving in the firelight attracted my attention. There was a shield, not three feet in diameter, rolling smoothly about the fire, decorated side out. Not until it had passed us and reached a point opposite us did I realize that Gordo was concealed behind it. As the shield rolled between us and the fire the second time, I could discern the toes of his moccasins — nothing else. He was loudly acclaimed.

Though we were in Juh's land, Grandfather presided as host upon this occasion. He stood to lead the cries for Mangus and for Naiche. Both were warmly received, and it was evident that both were pleased over the recognition. When they had taken their places Nana reminded the men that there was yet another great warrior to be honored. "She whom we had mourned as dead has returned to her people. Though she is a woman there is no warrior more worthy than the sister of Victorio. Come, my daughter."

Such acclaim went up that I did not know of her presence until she stood before Grandfather with bowed head and downcast eyes. At the renewed cheers Lozen wept. Obviously embarrassed she turned to leave, but Nana forbade it. He assured her that we respected her none the less for being a woman. Then he asked quietly if she would make Medicine to determine if an enemy were near.

The Woman Warrior stepped back and extended her arms, with her palms up and hands cupped. She stood with uplifted face and slowly revolved as she sang:

> Over all in this world
> Ussen has Power.
> Sometimes He shares it
> With those of this earth.
> This Power He has given me
> For the benefit of my people.
> This Power is good.
> It is good, as He is good.
> This Power I may use
> For the good of my people.

"No enemy is near," she said.
"For that we thank Ussen," said Grandfather.

Casas Grandes

To my great disappointment, we did not go to the mountain top of our dreams. Many of the women and children 'shared my reaction, but nobody protested. Had Grandmother been with us she might have influenced Nana, but no one else could. The three leaders decided to cooperate with each other in the useless struggle, and that settled the matter. They were to be united in their objectives, but not to stay together unless necessity required it, for that was the way of my people. In case of need, a runner went for assistance.

The young men were happy, for war was their life. We were essentially a hunting and a fighting people, and gloried in the fact. There was little probability that Mexican cavalry would invade Juh's fastness, nor that the Blue Coats would find it. Unless guided there by Chiricahua scouts they had not the resourcefulness to locate us. But in either event we needed ammunition, and much of it. Juh decided to make a trip to Casas Grandes, where he was accustomed to going for supplies. Grandfather knew well that the Mexicans plied his men with the fiery liquor they made, with the idea of getting them drunk and killing them. Sánchez urged Nana to go.

"We have nothing to trade to the Mexicans," was his objection, and a valid one.

"Why not go back to the arroyo where we buried the silver?"

[129]

To Grandfather that was preferable to Casas Grandes, and we went. How Nana could find his way through the pathless canyons and mountains has always seemed mysterious to me, but that ability was one reason for the confidence in which he was held. Kaytennae told me many times that he could not have led us there. He knew well that Nana feared the effect of the wealth upon the men, and was not eager to have them take it to Casas Grandes. And he wondered if Grandfather might not lead them to the wrong destination.

The place looked just as it had. There was still debris in the bed of the arroyo. Digging without shovels is slow and tiring. Both men and women used sticks and flat stones to scoop sand from the place. The silver had not been buried deep, but it might have sunk because of its weight. They should have found it three feet below the surface, but it was not there. They went on until only the heads of the workers showed above the walls, but without finding anything. When they struck a layer of stone they began another pit, a little above the first. There they found nothing; then they started a third, lower down the channel.

Was it possible that this was not the right place? The bar in the cottonwood! It was still there, just where Kaytennae had placed it. Could a flash flood have changed the course of the stream? They searched for evidence of one but did not find it. I think we must have been at that place more than a week before the young men gave up the search. Grandfather waited patiently, and he betrayed no satisfaction at their failure. Nevertheless, I think he was pleased.

We made a leisurely trip toward Casas Grandes, without encountering cavalry. Occasionally we passed near a lonely camp, or we heard a *carreta* moving slowly along the trail. The wheels were made of cross sections of a cottonwood log, with a hole burned in the approximate center for the axle. If they lubricated the axle with *nopal* leaves, it did not affect the sound which could be heard for miles. Nana strictly forbade his men to molest one of the vehicles, for Juh was on good terms with the Mexicans and did not want their enmity.

About three days' walk from Casas Grandes, we camped in a canyon which had obviously been used often for the purpose. A little stream trickled at the bottom of an almost perpendicular cliff. Fire-darkened stones lay in position for holding a cooking pot. It was a pleasant, safe retreat.

The next morning Kaytennae and Martine climbed to a ledge on the cliff. There they found the remains of a ladder. Using one of the poles they climbed higher and saw the small opening of what appeared to be a cave near the top of the rimrock. I thought of Grandfather's story of the hidden gold and was afraid. Gold is the seed of the Sun God and not to be desecrated. We watched them anxiously. They were unable to go higher without ladders, and they had none. They came to us as He Who Steals Love rode in and reported that he had sighted horsemen. We mounted and rode. If that were indeed the place about which Nana had told us, his secret died with him.

The horsemen, if there really had been horsemen, had disappeared and we saw no more of them. Possibly Grandfather was responsible for the warning, but a false report was a dangerous thing not only to the carrier of the message, but to every person in the tribe.

We moved along a river until we were close to Casas Grandes. We camped among trees with open glades on all sides. There the Mexican people brought green corn (roasting ears) and we feasted. Nana forbade anyone to go to the town, and sternly enforced that order. The women made *tiswin,* the mild, fermented drink to which we were accustomed. The men liked it, and could drink quantities without becoming intoxicated.[1] But they still had the craving for the mescal of the town.

Kaytennae told Grandfather of a little farm near Casas Grandes and of a family who had once tended him when he was wounded. The people had dressed his arm, given him food, and kept him overnight. He wished to go to that place, and would take Mother along. They would bring back a bag of green corn, they would not go to the town, and would remain only one night. I begged to be included but they arranged for me to stay with Martine's wife. As they rode away I slipped to the edge of the *bosque* and watched. The women in camp were burying the heads of cattle to bake for a feast and paying no attention to me. My parents rode across an open space toward more trees. I waited until they entered the grove and then set out after them. I saw their horses at the far edge of the timber and dropped to the ground. When I raised my head to look they were riding toward me. Kaytennae reached down and lifted me to the horse in front of him.

"Little Son, you have disobeyed."

"Yes, my Father."

"You know that disobedience can result in death?"

"Yes, my Father."

"Do you love your mother enough to risk your life to be with her?"

"You, too, my Father."

In silence they rode back to camp. All the way I wondered if Kaytennae would hit me with a stick. Apaches seldom strike children unless it is necessary to impress them sufficiently to prevent their risking their lives. But that I had done. I knew I deserved punishment, but thought it would be easier to die than to be beaten. In all my life nobody had laid a hand on me except in kindness.

Kaytennae dropped me at the arbor and unsaddled. Neither Kaytennae nor Mother seemed aware of my existence. Everybody ignored me. All afternoon I lived in dread of the whipping. If Nana had just glanced toward me one time I might have gone to him, but Grandfather had the ability of becoming remote when he chose. It was his disapproval I dreaded above all else. If I were beaten how could I ever face him again? It was not pain I feared but the humiliation of being beaten with a whip as were the people who submitted to slavery in the mines.[2]

The good odors of the evening meal came to me and the people took their seats about the fires. Mother did not call me. I could hear voices and laughter. I wanted to die. I lay face down with my hands over my ears until I went to sleep. When I awoke I was in the arbor, and it was a new world. My parents treated me as they had been accustomed to doing. Nobody mentioned either my disobedience, or my punishment. Grandfather was unusually kind. I faced Kaytennae and told him I was sorry. Without being asked I promised that I would never disobey them again.

We stole no horses in that country, for Nana did not wish to antagonize the people friendly to Juh. We turned our horses out to graze and each evening sent He Who Steals Love and Boy out to bring them to camp. When they were late once Kaytennae started to meet them. Ponce, whom I'd never seen before, returned with them. He told of having ridden upon the scene when two *vaqueros* were attempting to rope the boys. With their long lances they parried the throws. Meanwhile the Mexicans urged the boys to leave us and

join their own people. They refused. This incident reassured Kaytennae as to their loyalty, and their preference for living with us.
Most captives did refuse to return after being with Apaches even a
short time.

Ponce brought word of a small band of Chiricahuas having
come into Chihuahua with him. They had seen the light of a fire and
gone to investigate. There was a tent near it, but neither men nor
horses about. That was a contradictory situation, and he feared it
was a trap. Though he urged caution, his brother, Chinchi, was
determined to examine the tent, for they were in need of ammunition.
The others protested but could not prevent the attempt. Chinchi
crept cautiously, circled the fire, and approached the place from the
rear. They saw flashes of fire and heard shots. They waited a long
time, but could not find him in the dark.

Next morning they returned and found the tent gone. They
exercised much caution before venturing to find his body. It was
gone. They followed the trail of the cavalry to a plain where there
were great expanses of prickly pears. Along one of them the horses
had run, dragging his body through the cactus. Chinchi was literally
bristling with thorns. There are few things more painful, and his
suffering must have been agonizing.

They buried their brother.

Many years later Ponce visited me at Fort Sill. He told again of
that terrible thing. And he gave an account of his scouting at Casas
Grandes after he left us:

"I slipped into the village at night and found a building with a
wall all around the outside of the roof. I watched through a hole left
for shooting. All that day Juh's men caroused on liquor given them.
To my surprise Geronimo was with them, and so was Chato. Juh
and Geronimo were not as drunk as the rest, and they realized the
danger in time to rally their forces and get most of them out of town.
There were still a few in the *cantina* across the street. I do not know
how many. The Mexicans left it, a few at a time. When I saw the
bartenders come out I knew the Apaches inside were doomed. I lay,
helpless to aid, while they barricaded the door, ignited a chili bomb,
and threw it through a narrow slit in the wall. They closed that
opening with mud. You know how quickly the fumes kill."

"You were with them when Nana joined them, then."

"Yes. I watched the battle at the little cone-shaped hill."[3]

All told, I think there were not more than fifty, when the advance guard reported a troop of Mexican cavalry ahead. When the soldiers saw they were cut off from the mountain, they took refuge on the bare hill. Nana knew he had them.

The Mexicans began piling stones to form a crude barricade about the top of the cone. Within the barrier they took their horses. We lay across the canyon at about their level, scarcely out of rifle range from them. The young men were so eager to attack that they did not wait for a command but withdrew to the bushes and began stripping for battle. They returned with Kaytennae in the lead, and the stranger, Chato, following. I saw the disappointment in my father's face when Nana motioned him to sit beside him.

"You, Slender Legs, will lead the attack. It is for you to decide upon your method."

It was some time before we detected movements at the base of the hill.

"They've surrounded it," said Geronimo.

"Each lies behind a stone," said Juh.

"What do they intend to do?"

We had not long to wait. Slowly and gradually the stones were rolled up the hill, with the bodies of the men hidden behind them. The Mexicans had seen, and they were wasting ammunition with no hits. I recognized He Who Steals Love and pointed him out to Kaytennae. He smiled and nodded. I knew he was proud of the boy.

Those who fire from above have every advantage if they remain cool-headed and know how to use it. The Mexicans were panicky. They fired at the rocks but could not halt the slow movement up the slopes. Not a shot was fired by our young men.

"They want the horses!" said Juh.

"Enjuh!" grunted Nana.

"But slow!" commented Geronimo.

"By the time our men reach the top the Mexicans will be out of ammunition," said Nana. "The rest will be easy."

Slowly but surely the stones moved up the hill, gradually coming closer to each other as they went, until a comparatively level place was reached. Across it the men struggled desperately, for their bodies were exposed to fire. If the Mexicans had not been panicky they might have stopped them there. Again up on the slope, our men made short work of the finish. They began bantering each other over the division of the spoils. Slender Legs, as leader, had announced that the officer's mount was to be his, and that none of the horses were to be shot.

The Mexicans ceased firing.

"It's a trick!" said Geronimo.

"Slender Legs will realize it," replied Nana.

Our men moved in slowly, holding their fire. The Mexicans' horses plunged recklessly inside the walls. Suddenly the war cry was heard and Slender Legs led the charge over the wall. From all sides our men closed in. Few shots were fired, for the Mexicans were out of bullets and our men did not waste ammunition.

We saw Slender Legs leap to the back of the mount he had chosen; then we saw him crumple and slide to the ground. There had been one Mexican bullet.

There was no scalping, no mutilation. It was a dejected war party that bore his body to us and buried it. There was no victory dance, no speech.

$\mathcal{L}oco$

A messenger came to Nana. "Geronimo wants a council," he said.

"Bid him come," returned Grandfather, haughtily.

With Geronimo came the tall, handsome son of Cochise. Following them were Juh and his son Delzhinne. Grandfather courteously indicated places for all. Then Perico, Fun, and Eyelash arrived, and behind them, Chato. Nana invited the three to a seat near him, but ignored Chato. That insolent young man attempted to take his place next to Geronimo and was waved aside. The rebuff seemed wasted. He took a place at the end of the line, disregarding the fact that he had no right to attend the council. His presence was in a way a defiance of all three leaders. I could see that Kaytennae was angry, but Nana's face betrayed no emotion.

Mother had finished serving the food, and she took her place behind Nana, with me beside her. All sat in silence as Grandfather produced a small bag of herbs and with an oak leaf rolled a cigarette. Kaytennae brought a light from the fire for him. All waited reverently as Grandfather made Medicine. After he had sent puffs of smoke in each of the four directions and prayed silently, there was a long pause.

Grandfather asked the purpose of the meeting.

It was Geronimo who replied, "Summer is near. Already at San

[136]

Chief Loco led a band that belonged to Victorio's Warm Springs Apaches. This drawing was made by Loco's grandson.

Carlos people are dying of hunger, heat, and insects. When winter comes how many of Loco's people will still live?"

Grandfather shook his head.

"They are our brothers. They are your brothers, and mine. I was born at the headwaters of the Gila, as was Loco.

"Loco has nearly four hundred people with him. Of these seventy-five are warriors. How many will die during the heat?"

"Many," replied Nana.

"They will suffer for food. They will suffer from bad water and the bites of the insects with the long beaks. They will die of that terrible sickness that causes people to shake like leaves in the wind, and to burn one minute and freeze the next. The soldiers had tried to live in that place and could not. They put Loco's people there not to live but to die."

"True."

"Moreover, Loco belongs with his people. He is a Warm Springs Apache and he has by far the greater part of those who are still alive with him. Why should he not fight with you?"

"He has neither arms nor ammunition," replied Grandfather.

"I have caches that he may use."

"That is good," replied Nana.

There was prolonged silence broken by Chato. "Loco," he sneered, "is a woman!"

"Loco is a man and a warrior!" said Nana, sternly.

"*Enjuh!*" came in chorus from the men.

"He sits idle, drawing rations from the White Eyes while we do the fighting," continued Chato.

Grandfather spoke slowly, courteously, as to a child, "Each Apache decides for himself whether or not he fights. We are a free people. We do not force men to fight as the Mexicans do. Forced military service produces slaves, not warriors."

"*Enjuh!*" came in chorus from the council.

Nana looked at Geronimo, for Chato was of his band, and Geronimo was responsible for the intrusion of his man. Grandfather addressed his comments to Geronimo, ignoring the intruder.

"As chief, Loco was obligated to accept the decision of his band. He, himself, was convinced that further resistance was useless, even as was the great Cochise. Loco has given his word not to leave the reservation. He will not break that promise."

"He could be forced to leave," said Geronimo.

"If he refuses there will be the loss of many lives, for he has given his word."

"Always your people!" sneered Chato.

"Always my people," agreed Nana, softly.

"You, Broken Foot, do not fight. You win by ambush and strategy."

"There could be no higher praise," said Nana.

Geronimo grunted approvingly.

"I have seen Loco tested. A young officer came to us for

guidance in selecting a suitable place for White Eyes to imprison us on a reservation. Victorio deeply and earnestly wanted peace. He sent Loco under orders to protect the officer. He tended that boy as a grandmother does a child. He stationed one man at the horse's head and another at its tail when the White Eye ascended a slope.[1]

"Loco will not leave San Carlos unless forced to do so."

"That can be done," replied Geronimo, "but it may cost both him and us lives. But it will cost more if he remains during the summer. Loco is intelligent; except for trusting the word of the White Eyes he is not stupid. He, too, is acting for the interest of his people."

He turned to his subordinate. "You are ambitious, Chato. If you wish to become a chief learn first to think of your people; second, respect for your superiors."

Chato strode haughtily from the council.

"His chatter is of no importance," said Nana, "but the loss of a good fighting man is. And Chato is a fighter."

"He will fight with us so long as it is to his advantage," replied Geronimo. "I marvel at your patience with him.

"I respect your position," continued Geronimo. "Loco is your warrior since you took command of the Warm Springs. It is necessary that a competent man protect the helpless in our absence. All acknowledge your courage and ability. Will you take charge of those who remain here while we ride to San Carlos?"

"Gladly," replied Grandfather.

"Have you suggestions?"

"A feint at an ammunition raid while the main body of warriors rides to San Carlos. Distract the attention of the cavalry from the main purpose. Take Lozen and no other women, for you will be burdened with noncombatants on the return trip. Your success depends upon swiftness and surprise."

En route to Camp Goodwin the band stole no horses, killed no people. Early one morning they swooped down on Loco's camp and demanded that he come with them.

"We have no rifles, no ammunition," the wily chief replied.

"Then you have no defense," said Geronimo, "and you cannot be accused of breaking your word when forced to do so."

The Chiricahua Geronimo near his camp in the 1880s. Geronimo (left) is mounted, as is Naiche, son of Cochise. The child in arms on the left is Geronimo's son.

Within minutes Loco's band was on the march. In that short time word had reached the sub-agency, and police had been dispatched to prevent the outbreak. Police Chief Sterling met the band and ordered it to turn back. He lifted his rifle to fire at Loco and Sta lash shot him. His men fled.

● ● ●

Juh led the way through the creek valley into the valley of the San Francisco River. They turned toward Stein's Peak and approached it from the north. From this point they had a commanding view in three directions. They camped with a mountain at their backs, and an incline thickly studded with boulders to the north and east. Next day they moved south along the west side of the mountains.

They spent two nights at that place: Ussen had delivered them from bondage, and they were obligated to render thanks to Him according to their custom — with song and dance. Moreover, Loco's band was reunited with its people and their gratitude required ritual expression.[2]

Before they slept, women cut heads of mescal and put them in pits to bake.

The second evening came with no signs of pursuit. They danced and sang late that night. So long as no enemy came, one place was as safe as another. I was not present upon this occasion, but heard the story from many who were, and among them, Frank Gooday, a lifelong friend. Kaytennae confirmed the account, but did not mention the part he played. Gooday told how the festivities continued until almost morning. They planned to leave at dawn, provided the mescal had finished cooking. Day was beginning to show a faint light in the east when Gooday's mother summoned him to go with her and two young women to inspect the pits. The girls hurried ahead to pull out the long leaves left standing for testing. As one stooped a shot was fired and she fell across the pit. The other ran. Gooday pulled his mother to cover behind a boulder. The second girl fell. He was unarmed except for a knife; he crouched with it in hand, waiting.

The shots had come from the north. He knew that Apache scouts had led the cavalry. Unarmed people were running for horses, and hiding behind boulders. In the skirmish that ensued with the scouts, warriors flocked toward the north to repel the scouts and permit the women and children to climb to the summit. They would flee down the ridge, staying under cover as much as possible. The men withdrew slowly uphill to stop in a position better suited to repel the scouts. The cavalry following them had not yet arrived.

Kaytennae then discovered a totally unexpected foe approaching from the east. The others were so intent upon fighting that they were not aware of the new menace. My father called to the nearest men — two Navajos who had married into the tribe, and both responded. Kaytennae wore two ammunition belts. He snatched another from a fallen brave and ran down the slope followed by the Navajos. The three took cover and began firing at the Blue Coats dismounting at the edge of the widely strewn boulders.

The three were armed with Springfields. Kaytennae could load and fire faster than any other man I've seen. Both he and Fun were said to be able to dodge bullets. Father ran forward, dodging and twisting, loading and firing. So did the Navajos. The soldiers fell back, leaving their mounts, probably expecting a large force to follow the three. The younger Navajo boy fell. Kaytennae jumped upon a cavalry horse and circled to pick up the man whom he thought was wounded. He called to the Navajo to spring upon the horse as he rode by, but the boy could not make it. A second time he made the attempt and failed. Then he called to the Navajo to catch the horse's tail when it passed; both were carried to safety.

The other warriors had heard the shooting and were coming to the rescue. The soldiers fled, leaving half their horses. These my people salvaged, and then followed the women, overtaking them, mounting as many as the horses could carry, and crossing the valley to the next range. Their pursuers from San Carlos were not in sight.

They were so exhausted that again they took some rest. In midafternoon they slept two hours in an arroyo, and then resumed their flight. All that night they fled toward Mexico. Once in the Blue Mountains they could rest and rejoice, a free people again. In the land of Juh there would be no pursuit. Security and abundance would come in a short time. The horrors of San Carlos would fade.

Many tributes have been paid our leaders for their ability and courage, and I believe they were deserved. But I have always believed that had Grandfather led that raid, the outcome would have been much happier. Geronimo was clever and resourceful, and so was Juh. Loco has never received the credit Grandfather thought his due. Certainly not one of them anticipated an attack from the south. Even though they had, they probably could have done little about it. The fleeing women caught the aroma of coffee and thought they were approaching a camp of their own people. Instead they encountered a big force of Mexican cavalry. They turned back with the horses almost running them down. They took shelter in a deep, winding arroyo and began scooping out holes in the bank toward the soldiers. They put the children in these.

The warriors covering the retreat heard the shots and rushed forward. They, too, took to the arroyo. It was so deep they cut footholds in the side so they could step up and fire. The women distributed ammunition and loaded rifles. As the men came in with a bag of ammunition, the mule carrying it was shot, and it lay behind them, perhaps fifty feet out of reach. They felt that if they could hold out till night the ammunition might be recovered.

Bugle calls warned them when to expect a charge. Men sprang to the steps, fired, and sank back to reload. Women, too, used rifles. Cavalry came so close that one rider tumbled into the arroyo. Lozen, her head concealed by a screen of cactus, dropped a man with every shot. Three times the Mexicans charged before deciding that the Apaches were not to be dislodged by that means. They sent men on foot to fire into the length of the arroyo, but the bends afforded some protection. Adept as my people were in detecting movement, and expert in marksmanship, that was a tragic day. They had to make every bullet effective. Toward evening the Mexicans withdrew out of range, but their voices carried. They heard an officer say, "Geronimo is in that ditch. Go in and get him!"

They could not wait for dark to attempt to retrieve the ammunition. A man might wriggle toward it unseen, but in order to bring it back he would have to stand and become a target for the enemy. Loco undertook the trip and got halfway before a sniper sighted him. He fell upon his face and lay still. Even our people thought him dead. Juh shot the sniper and called to Loco to return. He had to do so without the bag.

Meanwhile the cavalry was lining up for the charge. There were cries of *"A Dios! A Dios!"* Then came the command and the horses thundered toward the arroyo. The Mexicans came very close before firing. They wheeled at the very brim to reform for another charge.

"Somebody get the ammunition. I'll hold them off till he gets back," screamed Fun. "When they charge, run for the bag."

The charge began and the dust blinded the Mexicans for the moment.

"Help me up the bank!" called a woman, and she ran, knife in hand, to cut the ammunition loose from the pack saddle. She could not lift the bag but started back, dragging it. Bullets whistled about her but she never faltered. As she neared the arroyo she stumbled and fell, but did not loose her hold. She extended her feet toward the ditch and the men pulled both her and the precious bag into it. Lozen got up calmly and began firing. Women distributed ammunition and men handed over empty rifles to be loaded.

During the charge, with his belt filled with bullets, and rows of them between his fingers, Fun sprang from the arroyo alone to meet the charge while Chihuahua, from a foothold, covered him. Dodging back and forth, Fun fired shot after shot at the advancing line. The cavalry may have expected others to follow him, for they wheeled and rode back. He jumped into the ditch for reloading. Before the Mexicans returned he was picking them off.

At dusk the last wave came, and again Fun met it alone. One man against many, miraculously dodging bullets! Perhaps my people are justified in believing that Ussen protects the brave. Before the dark closed down, the ammunition was almost gone. All knew that if they were to live they must flee to the mountains. Along the irregular line each little group obeyed the command of the nearest leader. Word was passed to leave the arroyo. The Mexicans anticipated this move and attempted to prevent it by setting fire to the vegetation. Flames crept toward the ditch.

Geronimo called to his men, "If we leave the women and children we can escape." Gooday told me that he could not believe that he had heard aright. Evidently Fun could not either for he faced his brother and said, "What did you say? Repeat that."

"Come on! Let's go."

Fun raised his rifle.

"Say that again and I'll shoot."

Geronimo climbed to the rim and disappeared. Men began

lifting children from the ditch and helping women scramble to the top. The clatter of hoofs warned them that another charge was upon them. *"Vaya con Dios!"* screamed the cavalry as it swept forward. Horses not dropped by bullets swerved at the very brink and riders tumbled into the ditch. Fun fired steadily until the children in his sector had been taken from the arroyo. Then the men, too, fled. Talbert Gooday and Dexter Loco stumbled over a baby. Gooday swept the child up and heard a voice call, "Duck in here!" He obeyed and found Chapo, son of Geronimo. They lay hidden until the pursuers passed. Both foot and horse soldiers ran down and killed our women and children.

During the night survivors assembled on a hillside, where Loco and Fun were attempting to rally their forces. When Gooday arrived with the infant, Loco took it in his arms and wept. It was his son. Geronimo and Juh had escaped in another direction. Kaytennae guided those who escaped to Nana. There Loco told Grandfather that costly as the fight had proved, a summer at San Carlos would have been more disastrous.[3]

Fort Apache

In one of our subsequent combinings of forces Juh's band camped with us. His wife was a wise and courageous woman. Juh had other wives and children, among whom were two grown sons and a married daughter. Geronimo's sister was Juh's favorite wife. Her son was perhaps four or five years older than I, and his name was Daklugie. There was a little girl about four. Apache children were seldom spaced closer than four years. Juh's camp was very close to ours. Both were near an arroyo which afforded concealment and exit in case of attack. We seldom assembled the forces because small bands could be more easily moved and concealed than large ones.

Early one morning the cavalry attacked. Kaytennae fought while Mother got the horses. She told me to run down the arroyo and that they would overtake me. As I passed Juh's shelter, burning arbors lighted it. I saw Ishton fall and her daughter dropped by a bullet beside her. The little girl was dead. Daklugie knelt beside his mother, and an older brother stood over them firing at the soldiers. I scrambled down the steep bank of the watercourse and soon heard hoofs behind me. Kaytennae bent and swept me to the saddle before him, and we reached the mountain safely.

Three days later Juh's sons carried their sister in on a stretcher made by fastening a blanket to two lances. She had been shot through the knee, and was a cripple thereafter. Daklugie's mother had died beside his little sister. Because they were relatives, Mangus kept the lad until after the Chiricahua went to Florida.

Chato had acquitted himself well in the disastrous flight of Loco's band from San Carlos. The cavalry gave our men credit for having fought like fiends to protect their helpless. Nobody questioned Chato's bravery, but nobody could be sure of his loyalty. After this disaster he left Geronimo and was temporarily attached to Chihuahua's band. Nana did not trust the young man and neither did Kaytennae. There was no open enmity but it was generally understood that Chato was a competitor for the chieftainship when Nana could no longer lead the Warm Springs. This our people resented not because he was a Chiricahua but because he was treacherous.

The White Eyes had no more implacable enemy than Chato. His brother had met death at their hands; so had their father, Mochas, and Chato boasted of having taken many lives in retaliation. With Chihuahua, Ulzanna, Tzoe (Bi-kli-tzoe), and several others he had raided New Mexico. The feat was daring and successful. The men rode hard, covered much territory, and killed many people. Judge and Mrs. McComas were slain, and their little son taken captive. I am often asked what became of that child. I do not know. I have heard several different accounts, all from reliable people. One thing I can say with certainty: had the warriors intended taking his life they would have done it when they killed the parents. Once having accepted him, they would have protected him as they did their own children. If he was killed during an attack on the Apaches he was one of many, and was given as much protection as could be afforded any other child. Daklugie said he had seen the boy, but did not know the manner of his death.[1]

Chihuahua and his raiders moved so rapidly that military officers thought two or more war parties were operating in New Mexico and Arizona. It was reported that Chato did not sleep except upon his horse. That is no doubt an exaggeration, but none of that band could have had much rest. When they swooped down toward San Carlos, Chihuahua lost a deserter. From that time Tzoe was called Yellow Wolf by our people in contempt for his treachery. The cavalry called him Tzoe, and never realized the contempt that name implied. The Coyote is the scheming, treacherous character of our folk tales, and the appellation is an insult. He was also called "Peaches" by the cavalry because of the color in his cheeks. In any event, Tzoe became a trusted scout.

Victorio had sternly forbidden his men to go into the villages of Mexico. Nana followed his example, though he was unable to prevent a few transgressions. Juh, on the other hand, made repeated trips to Casas Grandes, in spite of the men he had lost there.[2] The Mexicans feared Juh, and when he went, met him with protestations of friendship, sold him supplies, and gave him mescal. He did his trading before permitting his men to go into the *cantina*. It was said that both he and Geronimo let only half their warriors drink at one time. On this occasion Juh had taken his three sons with him, and he took the precaution to send his men ahead with his purchases before leaving the town. Satisfied that none remained in Casas Grandes he bade one of his sons overtake the warriors and deliver a message. Daklugie and Delzhinne (his sons) rode with him. Several miles out of Casas Grandes Juh's horse fell into the river. The banks were not high, the water not deep, and both boys reached him quickly. He lay in shallow water, apparently stunned by the fall. They were unable to lift the heavy man to the overhanging bank. Daklugie held his head above water while the older brother went for help. He was alive when the warriors returned. They built a shelter for him and tried to save his life, but he died shortly after. They buried him beside the river.

Disheartened by the death of their chief, even the Nednhi were willing to consider Loco's proposal to return to San Carlos before the cold of winter made the Sierra Madre forbidding. Neither Naiche nor Mangus had hopes of eventual success; neither had the desire to attempt the feats of his father, nor to suffer his fate. Many were expressing the fear that reservation life was inevitable and that further resistance could result only in the extermination of our people. Grandfather had always advocated death in preference to captivity. Geronimo shared his conviction. Both were shrewd enough to know that when they chose they could leave the reservation. Both felt that if they were under the supervision of the Department of War rather than that of the Interior they might receive humane treatment and be placed where living conditions were much better than at San Carlos. Nana learned that General Crook had been placed in charge of our area. This was good, Nana

Chato, a Chiricahua and a competitor for chieftainship of the Warm Springs tribe who suspected him of treachery. He later enlisted at San Carlos as a Scout.

thought. He was an enemy, yes, but he was an honorable enemy. His promise was good; his understanding of Apaches was fair.

Crook's scouts were in Sonora trying to reach us. Why not permit them to do so? If the young officer in command made a promise of supplies and a place acceptable to us, we would receive food, clothing, and supplies for the winter. We would be more comfortable than in the high Sierra. Also, we would not be subjected to the greed and thieving of a civilian agent. Besides — the stay need be only temporary. There would be another summer . . . . .

We needed horses badly for most of ours had been lost in the battle in the arroyo. Some had been killed for food, for we preferred their meat to beef. Besides, we had been unable to engage in our favorite sport — stealing horses. With the men lying in reserve, the boys dashed down upon a *remuda,* waved blankets and stampeded it toward the warriors. How I longed to ride with them! But I was not yet old enough. Daklugie went, and how I envied him! The party returned with few horses, but driving a herd of cattle. Nana was disgusted. Handicapped by the slow-moving animals, we were greatly retarded. Geronimo reminded Grandfather that regardless of promises, fulfillment was difficult; and that, after all, beef also was edible.

Through Lozen and Dahteste, the chiefs opened negotiations with Lieutenant Britton Davis, and arranged for a meeting. Geronimo sent word to Chihuahua. Mangus, too, was notified, but did not come. Chato went to San Carlos and and enlisted as a scout. Chato!

The council was held. Lieutenant Davis promised that if we came in we would be permitted to live on Turkey Creek not far from Fort Apache. *Enjuh!* That country was to our liking — mountainous, with streams, timber, game, and privacy. Nana and Geronimo agreed to go. The young officer protested taking the cattle. Grandfather did not commit himself but Geronimo refused to go in without them.

Just across the border in Arizona we stopped at an adobe house by a spring. Because of our cattle, we had moved slowly, and had eaten lots of dust. We suffered for water. We were so exhausted that Lieutenant Davis promised Geronimo a three-day rest at that spring before going to San Carlos.

Once across the line we no longer needed dread attack by the

Dahteste, a Chiricahua, had been on the warpath with Geronimo. With Lozen, noted Medicine Woman of the Warm
Springs Apache, she acted as go-between for Apache leaders
and American military officers attempting to resolve some of
their conflict of purpose.

Mexican cavalry, and with the young officer in charge we were protected from the Blue Coats. We could sleep without fear of attack. And we could rest before resuming the march.

We camped around the spring, and all about the house. Toward night two White Eyes rode in and went to Lieutenant Davis. One was an officer. Yanosha, who knew many English words, and I scouted and overheard them discussing the cattle. One man said he was from the Customs and he wanted to take our cattle because we had not paid any tax on them. Our cattle! He hadn't stolen those cattle; why should he get them?

The other was from Tucson, an officer, but not in the Army. Blue coat, though. And he didn't want anything but Geronimo! He had some kind of a piece of paper to bring Geronimo in and put him in jail. And why? Just because Geronimo fought to protect his family, his tribe, and his land! What kind of a man is it that won't fight for those?

Davis went to Geronimo. The chief was very angry. He reminded the young officer of his promise, and of the trust placed in him. This, Davis said, was something beyond his control.

While they were talking, a third White Eye came, and he was an army man who outranked Lieutenant Davis. The two conferred. The newcomer took bottles from his saddlebags, and the two went into the house with the others. There was much drinking, and finally the Customs man and the Tucson policeman went to sleep. The third man stayed with them, but Britton Davis came to Geronimo. If the Apaches were still about in the morning, when those men awoke, Geronimo would be put in prison. The cattle would be taken from us. And the Apaches might have to be put back in Mexico.

Of course, moving that number of people, to say nothing of the cattle, was simply impossible. Nobody could get them up and on the march without waking those men. Dogs would bark, children would cry — there was just nothing to do but for Geronimo to go to jail . . . . .

If any people knows how to be quiet it is the Apache. If anybody can control his children and his women, and his horses and dogs, it is the Apache. But the cattle!

We shook with laughter as we got everything ready to move. It did not take ten minutes. Not a dog barked. Not a baby cried.

We tied children's feet together under the bellies of the horses. We tied small children to adults. And we started. At first we moved slowly, very slowly. We had to, because of the cattle. But after we got out of hearing we put boys with lances to keep the cattle moving, and we made time. By morning we were far north of that spring — maybe twenty miles.

General Crook met us at San Carlos. It was not summer yet, and the men were willing to stay there till they got the promised supplies. They were assured that the Lieutenant's promises would be kept. We were to go to Turkey Creek as soon as the equipment could be got ready.

Then came Mexican officers looking for those cattle. They examined the brands and claimed them — every one of our cattle they claimed. And General Crook let them take them. We were beginning to be very sorry we had come.

Nana went to the General who tried to explain why he took our cattle, but it was hard to understand. Nobody did understand. But Nana felt better when General Crook told him we were to have breeding stock, both cattle and sheep, for our own use. We were to have tools with which to raise food, too, but for that we did not care. General Crook had recommended livestock as a source of income, but the ignorant men in Washington wished to make farmers of us. We must plow and plant. The young officers who had been with us realized how stupid that was, but could do nothing about it.

Lieutenant Cruse wrote, "These Indians are not agricultural. They were men who from the dawn of history had ranged constantly over the rugged country, killing their food. To them freedom was life."

Had the money spent for wagons, plows, and implements whose use we did not know been put into cattle we might have been content indefinitely on Turkey Creek. Instead we received the useless things which somebody in Washington considered necessary for our existence. We knew nothing of wagons. The harness that we received was made for draft horses, and the collars were so large that our ponies could almost crawl through them. There were pieces of that equipment strung all the way from San Carlos to Fort Apache. We could have made the trip much more swiftly and easily without it, but we really tried to get it to the fort.[3]

Turkey Creek

From the beginning my people spoke of Lieutenant Britton Davis by his given name. They liked him because of his helping Geronimo get his people away from the officers. They liked him for many other reasons. He was a western man, albeit a graduate of West Point, and I believe his father was at one time governor of Texas. Above all he seemed to like and understand Apaches. I think that when Caesar went into Britain he found the inhabitants in about the same stage of advancement that we were at this time. There was a gap of two thousand years to bridge, but the young officer was able to comprehend most of our mental processes. It may be true that peoples do not differ materially in their psychology, but they certainly do in some of their mores.

Britton Davis had the great advantage of not being a civilian agent. I know there have been honest and conscientious ones, such as James A. Carroll who was with the Mescaleros many years later. But we had never known that kind, and not even the white people at that time could believe in the integrity of the Apache agent. Some of the officers were hard on us, but they were not thieves. We knew that the food provided for our use would be dispensed to us by the Army.

So we went with confidence to that place some twenty miles from Fort Apache — about five hundred of us, including perhaps

[154]

seventy-five warriors. We were described as being as dangerous men as the world had ever produced. With us went this young White Eye, Nantan Davis. He took with him two interpreters, both of whom the Chiricahua had good cause to hate. Can anybody think that if our chiefs had wished to have Britton Davis killed that Mickey Free would have been of any help to him? Of Sam Bowman we were not at first sure, but we knew that Mickey Free was incapable of loyalty.

Sam Bowman was part Cherokee and knew enough of our language to interpret fairly well. We learned that he could be trusted to convey our meaning honestly. But because Mickey spoke our language fluently he was usually used for interpreting. He was a half-breed — a thing abhorrent to Apaches. He had, through no fault of his own, been the cause of Cochise's outbreak. Though the trouble was precipitated by the ignorance and arrogance of a young officer, it was occasioned by the abduction of Mickey Free by other Apaches than Cochise's men, and indirectly the child was held to be responsible. Moreover, the Chiricahua considered him to be treacherous and unreliable.

It is a terrible thing for the fate of an inarticulate people to depend upon the spoken word of a renegade with no whit of integrity. My people knew well how an ambitious young lieutenant sought to arrest Cochise by inviting him to a tent for a conference. That was none other than Lt. George Nicholas Bascom. Once inside with some of his people Cochise realized that he was surrounded by troops. An experienced old sergeant went to the officer and protested against the treachery and stupidity of his commanding officer and was courtmartialed for insubordination. The chief cut his way through the tent and escaped, but his wife, his infant son, Naiche, and his two brothers were held. The wife and child were released, but the men were hanged.[1]

For ten years Cochise exacted vengeance.

Now the Chiricahua were at the mercy of the coyote whose kidnapping had brought war to the Chiricahua. Knowing that he would twist their words and discredit them, the Apaches refrained from contact with Lieutenant Davis unless summoned by him. It was apparent to them that Britton trusted Mickey Free, and that he employed him to interpret when he was present. When they had to go to the officer they tried to find a time when Sam Bowman could act for them. Neither they nor Bowman could explain to Davis that they distrusted Mickey. So the invisible curtain prevented friendly overtures.

They were thankful when Britton Davis moved his headquarters to Turkey Creek. He pitched his tent on the east side of the stream, opposite the brush arbors of Kaytennae and Nana.

Chihuahua and Mangus were within a few minutes' walk of us. But Geronimo and Naiche camped some distance away, with their warriors close. All cultivated little open glades and planted corn and vegetables. There was an abundance of good water, wood, and game. There was good grazing. There were no mosquitoes, few rattlesnakes, and no cavalry. There were poles and brush to make shelters, and even the canvas of old tents for covering them until hides could be secured. The only use I remember for wagons was to place the beds on the side toward the wind for shelter. In addition, we planted rows of evergreens around the arbors to serve as windbreaks.

We learned at San Carlos that the report of Chato's enlisting as a scout was true. Many were being recruited, and Chato invariably allied himself with what he thought would be the winning side. Some good and loyal Chiricahua had served as scouts, and several of them reenlisted at the time. There was never any question of Chihuahua's devotion to his people, and he had gone back into the service. So had Rogers Toklanni. Ours was a race of fighting men — war was our occupation. A rifle was our most cherished possession. And though the scouts were permitted to have only five bullets at a time, and had to account for each one fired, a weapon is a weapon. And, believe me, there was not a man who did not envy the scout his rifle.

Again the sound of The Morning Song arose from the arbors. One morning as Grandfather sang I heard him snort indignantly and Kaytennae rushed to his shelter.

"Chato!" he grunted. "There!"

It was indeed Chato. Bound about his forehead was the red cord of the scouts. He wore a shirt of government issue; like the rest he had an ammunition belt and carried a rifle, but wore breech clout and moccasins. Nana went to Geronimo and after their conference several of our men who had previously refused to enlist went into the scouts. Among them were Perico, half-brother to Geronimo, and Chapo, the latter's son. Davis kept a good many with them, with

Chato as first sergeant, and Juan second. Chapo became the lieutenant's orderly. All could speak Spanish, but unfortunately the
young officer did not. All picked up English rapidly, but could not
speak it as well as necessary to dispense with an interpreter.

Davis urged Kaytennae to enlist, and assured him of rapid promotion if he should. My father courteously declined. He, Nana,
Geronimo, and Naiche avoided contact with the officer and the
scouts. They sent the women of the families to draw rations. Let
Chihuahua and Toklanni be gullible if they wished. Let them carry
rifles and wear ammunition belts if they chose. Did not Nana and
Geronimo have hidden weapons and ammunition? What were five
bullets?

How could tried and true warriors be deceived by the trickery
and conniving of Mickey Free and Chato? Let them see for themselves — in time they would. But let them understand meanwhile
that they had forfeited the respect of their people.

We raised corn, squash, pumpkins, pinto beans, and other
vegetables. We especially liked roasting ears. We had not recently
stayed anywhere long enough to plant corn, but had got some from
the Mexicans near Casas Grandes. Then there was another food, an
oblong thing larger than a turkey egg, and covered with thin brown
skin. Mother roasted it in the ashes. We liked potatoes. And how we
enjoyed watermelon! Britton Davis did, too. When Mother sent
me with one I crossed by the foot log to his tent with it. He gave
me a tin can with a picture of a beautiful red food on it. When
Mother opened the can she threw the tomatoes out, because the
paper was a ghost thing. My people feared that a reproduction of
any natural object might displease Ussen who made no two things
identically. Many thought that if we ate the contents of a can we
might be witched, though they knew that Apaches could not witch
White Eyes. Whether the reverse was true they did not know.

Britton Davis ate the flesh of turkey, too. And he gave us sugar
in exchange for catching mountain trout for him. He ate pork every
morning — we could smell the tantalizing odor of bacon. But because turkeys and wild hogs devour snakes, no Apache would eat
their flesh.

Mother hoarded the cans to make the little tin jingles used on
ceremonial garments.

Once I came in with a flat container upon which was pictured
the figure of a tall thin man with hooves and a tail. The officer had

been eating man meat! My people had been told that sometimes White Eyes practiced cannibalism, and here was the proof. No more collecting of discarded cans! Nana made Medicine for me and I suffered no ill effects.

Kaytennae taught the boys to play the hoop and pole game. He was very skillful at it, and those who gambled upon him usually won. It is played with long, peeled poles, slender and straight. At the blunt end, buckskin bands are bound at intervals for counting the score. The hoop is usually made of willow, carefully rounded, and the ends secured with sinew. The hoop is laced across with buckskin thongs running parallel to one crossing the center. The contestants stand at one end of a smooth, level space with their poles. In turn they throw at a hoop rolled from the other end toward them. When it begins to lose momentum the contestant tries to gauge the exact spot and instant it will topple to the ground, and to throw his pole so that it will fall across the banded end. If the middle thong of the hoop falls across the pole a perfect score is made, but that is almost impossible. Both the bands and the thongs are considered in computing the score.

My father trained us also in the use of primitive weapons. The sling was my favorite. He made one for me that he could use effectively at a hundred yards. Stones are good weapons in the hands of an accurate thrower, and when hurled from a sling they can be deadly. The boys of our band liked to engage in mock battles with those of the White Mountain and Tonto Apaches. We sometimes encountered them in the evening when we went for the horses. We scouted for sign, and each tried to ambush the other. When hostilities began, each advanced toward the other, dodging and twisting to prevent being hit, and making use of such cover as we could. If we were greatly outnumbered we sent for reinforcements, and at times men joined us. I know of one such encounter at Mescalero in which a leg was broken, and a neck dislocated so that its owner went through life with his head held to one side. That was Crook Neck. Once I got a glancing blow above the eye. It did not cut deep, but I was ashamed to go home, and did not get in till after dark. Next morning I saw Mother and Kaytennae exchange glances but neither mentioned my wound.

Mangus lived near us, and with him Istee and Daklugie. Kaytennae took them under his tutelage, as well as He Who Steals Love, and Boy. Others sometimes joined us. Occasionally Father took us hunting, using bows and arrows. If we got far enough from camp that there was little danger of discovery, he permitted us to practice with his rifle. He knelt behind me to hold the weapon, but let me sight and pull the trigger. Scarcity of ammunition prevented much practice with firearms.

Every day Kaytennae made us bathe, though in winter we had to break the ice to plunge into the stream. We built a fire on the bank and left our breech clouts and moccasins by it. Back and forth we went, from icy water to fire. But nobody had a cold, nobody got sick. Illness was unknown.

The older people bathed frequently just as they required us to do. In the desert where water was unobtainable they rubbed their bodies with sand. White people may not regard the soil of the earth as clean, but until it was polluted it was free of germs that cause infection. Smudges of earth are not as injurious as immaculate-looking substances contaminated with disease.

During those months at Turkey Creek dawn was greeted with The Morning Song. We were grateful to Ussen for comparative safety both from enemies in the military sense and from the greed and cruelty of Indian agents. The supplies General Crook promised were issued to us by Britton Davis. It has always seemed to me that the Army was much fairer in its treatment of us than the Department of Interior. We knew that our brothers at San Carlos were being robbed by the agent and their food and blankets sold at Globe. We knew, too, that many were unjustly imprisoned.

Except for the influence exercised by Chato and Mickey Free over Britton Davis, we had little difficulty. Food, clothing, and shelter are considered basic human needs. We had those, and we had also a fourth — that of worshipping Ussen according to our ancient custom. We expressed our gratitude by prayer, song, and dance. My people had a strong compulsion to do so, and they valued the privilege.

They kept their promises so well that General Crook wrote "From the time of my arrival until March, 1883, there were no depredations committed by Indians, either reservation or renegade, in Arizona."

As early as October, 1882, a federal Grand Jury indicted Agent Tiffany of San Carlos. It charged that "He had kept eleven men in confinement for fourteen months without charges or any attempt to accuse them, knowing them to be innocent."

The indictment stated further: "For several years the people of this Territory have been gradually arriving at the conclusion that the management of the Indian Reservation in Arizona was a fraud upon the Government; that the constantly recurring outbreaks of the Indians and their consequent devastations were due to the criminal neglect or apathy of the Indian Agent at San Carlos; but never until the present investigations of the Grand Jury have laid bare the infamy of Agent Tiffany could a proper idea be formed of the fraud and villainy which are constantly practiced in open violation of the law and in defiance of public justice. Fraud, peculation, conspiracy, larceny, plots, and counterplots seem to be the rule of action upon the reservation. The Grand Jury little thought when they began this investigation that they were about to open a Pandora's box of iniquities seldom surpassed in the annals of crime.

"With the immense power wielded by the Indian agent almost any crime is possible. There seems to be no check upon his conduct. In collusion with the chief clerk and storekeeper, rations can be issued *ad libitum* for which the Government must pay, while the proceeds pass into the capacious pockets of the agent. Indians are sent to work in the coalfields, superintended by white men; all the workmen and superintendents are fed and frequently paid from the agency stores, and no return of the same is made. Government tools and wagons are used in transporting goods and working the coalmines, in the interest of this closed corporation and with the same result. All surplus supplies are used in the interest of the agent, and no return made thereof. Government contractors, in collusion with Agent Tiffany, get receipts for large amounts of supplies never furnished, and the profit is divided mutually, and a general spoilation of the United States Treasury is thus effected. While six hundred Indians are off on passes, their rations are counted and turned in to the mutual aid association, consisting of Tiffany and his associates. Every Indian child born receives rations from the moment of its advent into this vale of tears, and thus adds its mite to the Tiffany pile. In the meantime, the Indians are neglected, half-fed, discontented, and turbulent, until at last, with the vigilant eye peculiar to the savage, the Indians observe the manner in which the

Government, through its agent, complies with its sacred obligations.

"This was the united testimony of the Grand Jury, corroborated by white witnesses, and to these and kindred causes may be attributed the desolation and bloodshed which have dotted our plains with the graves of murdered victims. *Foreman of the Grand Jury.*"

Captain Bourke, in *On The Border With Crook,* said:

"The rations doled out had shrunk to a surprising degree; one shoulder of the small cattle of that region was made do twenty people for a week; one cup of flour was issued every seven days to each adult. . . . Spies were sent upon the agency who followed the wagons laden with Indian supplies to Globe and the other towns just named, to which they traveled at night, there to unload and transfer to the man who purchased from the agent or his underlings. . . . The rottenness of the San Carlos Agency extended all the way to Washington, and enfolded in its meshes officials of high rank."

The crimes of the agents were well known to the Apaches, but they did not know at that time that any White Eye had ever raised a protesting voice in their behalf. They were both illiterate and inarticulate. They were completely at the mercy of their keepers. Is it strange that they appreciated the young officer who had them in charge in spite of the fact that he made an error in judgment in his choice of confidants?

I have talked with many other old people of my race who regard Britton Davis as one of the best men ever put in charge of us. To this day the older Apaches believe that Davis resigned his commission because he became aware of the deceit practiced upon him by Mickey Free and Chato.

Kaytennae

Few Apaches have been critical of Britton Davis for the arrest of Kaytennae. They knew Davis was influenced by the reports that came to him through Chato, Mickey Free, and Tzoe. Chato had always been jealous of my father, and particularly after he came to the realization that Kaytennae would undoubtedly succeed Nana as chief. With the aid of Mickey Free and Tzoe, Chato convinced Davis that my father was rebellious and planning to lead the young men in a revolt from the reservation.

Had the lieutenant questioned his old and tried scouts — Chihuahua, Tissnolthos, and Toklanni — he would have heard a different story. Errors in judgment are understandable. Sometimes the more honorable the individual the more difficult it is for him to believe in the perfidy of others. Perhaps some men would have gone to the officer and warned him, but not an Apache. Chihuahua, in particular, had reason to distrust Chato. He learned that the officer had spies who went to his tent at night. Chihuahua lay hidden outside and heard a pebble hit the canvas. At that signal the young man admitted Chato, and a little later another pebble against the tent was followed by the arrival of three more — one of whom was a woman. Did an honorable scout go to make his report stealthily, and in the company of spies, one of them a woman? Chihuahua lay against the canvas while Mickey Free and Chato fabricated a story of Geronimo's and Kaytennae's attempts to incite an uprising. Mickey Free! That miserable little coyote was trusted, and old and honest scouts disregarded. Chato! Turncoat and traitor!

The next morning Chihuahua presented himself to the officer. Mickey Free undertook to interpret and Chihuahua ordered him to close his mouth with its forked tongue.[1] He called for Sam Bowman and through him spoke to Britton Davis: "I have served as scout many years longer than Chato. I have served faithfully and told no lies. All that I have reported has been true; and there is proof of my faithfulness. I have told no lies. I have not sneaked to your tent at night. But I am not a spy and I will not work for anyone who employs one."

"How do you know what Chato has told me?" asked Davis.

"I heard. I do not speak much English, but I understand. He told you that Geronimo and Kaytennae are plotting an outbreak. He told you that I am planning to kill you and go with them. Had I wished to do that I could have done so long ago."

Chihuahua removed his military equipment, and threw rifle, head band, ammunition belt, and shirt in a heap in the corner.

"Take this stuff and give it to your spies."

"You can't quit," said Davis. "You've just reenlisted. You have a long time yet to serve."

"I am quit," said Chihuahua. And he stalked indignantly out of the tent. He did not report for duty again. He remained quietly in his camp, constantly expecting arrest, but it did not come. He called the chiefs together. They listened. Perico, Chihuahua said, could verify his account. So could Chapo. Geronimo nodded.

"They have done so already."

"One of these spies is a woman."

"I know."

"And you permitted this?"

"It was one sure way to learn of Chato's treachery. Nana knew. Kaytennae knew."

"Then why wasn't I told?"

"My brother is honest and loyal, but he is hasty."

"When I see treachery I speak."

"That quality all respect. This White Eye is young. In many ways he has done well. In time he will learn to judge people and not be deceived by people like Chato."

"And I have antagonized him unnecessarily."

"Perhaps not. Chato will be so eager for promotion that the officer will think of what you have said. Once he gets suspicious he will find proof."

"Does Chapo know?"

"I told him nothing, for Chapo lacks years. But he has long suspected that Chato was working against Kaytennae, and has warned me."

"What can we do?"

"Wait."

They did not wait long. The men congregated at our camp to play the hoop and pole game. Kaytennae and Mangus were competing, and because both were expert the betting was high. Nana sat on a blanket with me on one side and Daklugie on the other. I was proud of my father's skill, and resentful when Nana sent me to Mother for water. When Grandfather lifted the jug Kaytennae laid his pole down and joined us. As Father stooped Nana murmured, "Soldiers behind the tent."

"I'll try!" said Kaytennae, loudly, and he returned to the game.

Then Mangus came for a drink.

"Rifles and ammunition in my arbor," said Nana, softly.

Across the little stream stood Britton Davis and a group of scouts, watching. Suddenly Chato and Mickey left them and went to the line where Kaytennae stood poised for his throw. Chato arrogantly ordered him to report to the officer. He nodded and smiled, with his eyes on the rolling hoop. He lifted the pole, gauged his distance carefully, and tossed the stick toward the toppling hoop. The ring lurched and settled upon the pole with the center thong lying upon it.

"He wins!" called Mangus. *"Enjuh!"*

Kaytennae walked leisurely across the log to the tent and stood talking with Britton Davis. He returned and sent He Who Steals Love for his horse. Mother asked no questions but prepared food and rolled a blanket.

"I'm called to San Carlos for a council. I'll return as soon as it's finished."

I saw a question in Nana's eyes, and it frightened me. Kaytennae mounted his horse, thanked the Mexican boy, and rode away with two scouts.

A troop of cavalry was in the timber behind the officer's tent. They came with orders that Kaytennae be sent to San Carlos. It was obvious that Chato and Mickey Free knew of their mission because they were unusually arrogant. Ostensibly the troops had come for the purpose of searching our camps for Mexican captives. They found and took several women, not one of whom went with them willingly. Grandfather rode with the cavalry and was able to prevent Chihuahua's son from being claimed because of his Mexican descent. Eugene was about eight years old, I think, and like his father, very light-skinned. The family told the men that the child was theirs, and Mother told them that she was present when Eugene was born. Even then the soldiers were skeptical. All this occurred while He Who Steals Love rode with Nana, and not one of them suspected that he was a Mexican. Finally Nana said, "Both Chihuahua and his son are light-skinned, but they cannot help that. Do not White Eyes and Mexicans also vary in color? I remember when that child was born. I remember when Chihuahua was born. They are true Apaches — not coyotes."

Late one night Toklanni came to Grandfather. Kaytennae was being held on a charge of inciting an uprising. He was not to have a trial* but to be sent to prison on an island in San Francisco Bay. He was to stay there five years. Five years! When Grandfather told us, Mother made no sound, but I buried myself in my blanket and tried to stifle my uncontrollable shaking and sobbing. Grandfather did not rebuke me. He sat beside me with head bowed and hand on my shoulder. I knew that Kaytennae was as his right hand, and that he suffered as did Mother and I.

After our evening meal she asked quietly, "Chato?"

"And Mickey Free. Both are jealous of Kaytennae. If Chato had not given up all hope of the men's selecting him in preference to Kaytennae he would never have become a scout. He knew well that he stood no chance."

"Will my father come back?" I asked.

"That I do not know. He may. After all, the White Eyes are not the Creators of the Earth, but Ussen is. He may permit Kaytennae to return to his people."

"Why did Ussen permit this thing?"

---

*There was a trial of sorts. Kaytennae was not present.

"That we do not know, and it is not for us to question His act. We can pray for Kaytennae's return, and we will."

"It is impossible," said Mother.

"With Ussen nothing is impossible. There was a time that I doubted, but I do so no more. I have seen many things happen that could have come about only by His will."

We waited.

"There was the spring in the Malpais when we fled to the Sacred Mountain. When I bent to get water Ussen warned me that it was unfit to drink."

"How, Grandfather?"

"He spoke in my ear. He speaks to all who listen."

"Again, when we saw the dust of Hatch's troops so close that it seemed impossible that the scouts would not find us before we could hide I heard His voice again. And again we were permitted to live. A scout passed within a stone's throw of where I lay. Not a dog barked; not a child cried; not a horse snorted. Do you think that happened by accident?"

Deep in my heart I knew that Grandfather was right, but I missed Kaytennae. How would Mother and I get along without him? She reminded me gently that we had once, and that when I was small enough to be a charge to her. Now I was a big boy who could defend her and take my father's place as a hunter. She reminded me that his rifle and ammunition were hidden in a safe place, and that if necessary I was to use them.

The arrest caused unrest and resentment among my people. They hated Chato and Mickey; and they expected that at any minute Chihuahua, Geronimo, Naiche, Grandfather, and Mangus might be placed under arrest. Grandmother sent me alone for the rations and Chato told me that Kaytennae was chained on a rock so far from land that no man could swim across that water.

Grandfather listened. "You know well that he is a liar. There is no water so wide but that Kaytennae can swim across it. I have traveled far and seen all the rivers in the land."

"But his wrists are chained."

"Last night while you slept I went to the Mountain to pray. I made Medicine. Ussen spoke. Kaytennae is to return."

I was comforted.

"And now, I have other proof of Ussen's goodness. You have a little sister."

I loved her as I had Chenleh, lost at Tres Castillos. I helped care for her, for Mother was busy preparing food for the winter. With several other families she was to move near Fort Apache. Food was to be issued us there, and in that valley we would avoid the long rides in cold weather for rations. He Who Steals Love went with us, but Boy remained with Grandfather. I could not lift a saddle to a horse's back, but fortunately we had a loyal and trustworthy helper in the Mexican boy. We loaded all our horses could carry and Mother mounted with the baby in her *tsach*.

Near the fort we built another brush arbor, and we had hides enough to cover it. We were about twenty miles from Grandfather, but had friends about us.

There was another blow: cavalry came with Mexican soldiers looking for captives. They put in a claim for He Who Steals Love and for Boy. Again they tried to take Chihuahua and Eugene. Grandfather was summoned and brought before the commanding officer. Never had I known Nana to lie, but I hoped that he might this time.

Nana did not come to us until after dark and he came alone.

$\mathcal{T}$he Return of the Women

Mother took the baby and went into the building to get our allotment of food. I stood outside, waiting. There was a cloud of dust in the east, but we did not fear dust as we had. I watched it increase in size and suddenly I wondered if it might not be caused by cavalry coming to arrest Grandfather. Each time a chief appeared, Mickey and Chato drew their hands significantly across their throats. They kept the leaders constantly expecting that they would be taken and their heads cut off.

Through the trees I got glimpses of blue-clad riders. Two! There was a wagon following them. Then more Blue Coats. As they drew near I saw that a soldier was driving, with his horse tied to the wagon. Two women sat in the seat, and three on the floor of the vehicle. The horses wheeled toward the door of the building and the wagon stopped. Cavalry, but none wore the insignia of officers. A man dismounted and courteously helped the women to the ground. As each stepped down to the hub the cavalryman held her arm until she got to the ground. The women were ragged and miserable looking, with black shawls like those worn by Mexican women over their heads. They had pieces of cowhide tied to their feet. The last to descend was very old. Her hair was white. My heart leaped within me.

"Grandmother!" I called as I ran to her.

[168]

She looked at me blankly.

"I'm Kaywaykla, Grandmother, I'm Kaywaykla!"

"You are a big boy. He was small."

"It's been a long time. I've grown."

She took me in her arms. Then another embraced me, and I drew back to look at her. Siki! The soldiers watched as I brought Mother to them. There were five, but I did not know the others. We started for our camp and Mother gave them food. Grandmother asked if Nana were living, and Mother sent a boy for him. Nobody slept till he arrived.

Where Huera and the others slept I do not know, but they must have found refuge with those whom they knew. Later Huera married; what became of the others, I do not know.[1]

Neither Grandmother nor Siki talked of that terrible night at Tres Castillos until Nana questioned them. Grandmother had run after my cousin to protect her from the soldiers. She pulled her blanket over her white hair because the aged were usually killed. She saw Siki dragged from her horse and tied to a scrubby tree. Before she could reach the girl Grandmother, too, was seized and bound. With her eyes she warned Siki to give no sign of recognition. As women and boys were dragged near the fire the guards separated those who attempted to communicate.

Grandmother's account follows:

The fighting was soon over, for our men had little ammunition. There was little cover available for our men. When they ceased fire we knew that they had either been killed or would be shortly. Next morning we learned that Victorio and three others had used their last bullets in defense of their people and then died by their own hands. The cavalry scattered to run down and kill those who had fled. The pursuit and slaughter of the helpless women and children continued for hours. Soldiers raced back and forth, beating the bushes, dragging the helpless from their hiding places, and killing them. Several boys were brought in — mostly half-grown ones. The younger women were kept. I thought that when morning came I would be killed. For the others — the slave market.

Toward morning a Lipan scout — Big Water — came in bringing a wounded officer. He recognized me and ordered me to dress the wound. When he cut the sleeve away I saw that the arm had been shattered by a bullet. The wounded man lay still while I bound prickly pear to the torn flesh and made a sling to support the arm. He gave orders that I was not to be killed.

While I was dressing the wound I learned from Big Water that he and another Lipan had been captured and compelled to lead the cavalry to the lake. Had they known that Victorio was taking refuge there they might have been able to avoid the place, but they thought him in the mountains to the west. Big Water told me that the cavalry horses had been ridden down, and that if our people had not dismounted and turned their horses loose they should have been able to escape. He said the Mexicans had no scouts except himself and the other Lipan. I had finished and could ask no more questions.

There were about a hundred captives, and among them fifteen young boys. Nobody was given food and water until past midday; the lads got nothing. When the order came to cut them loose they knew well what was in store for them. One of the older ones said to the rest, "They take us now to the brush to kill us. Let us remember that we are Apaches and show them how men can die!" With heads held high they walked proudly ahead of the guards.

Then came the shots.

That evening a messenger from the city of Chihuahua came with orders to kill no prisoners. I was released to attend the wounded officer and I heard. Next morning, driving us ahead like cattle, the cavalry started to the City of Mules. Those unable to keep up with the line of march were shot. Siki was so frightened and so exhausted that I feared that at any time she might fall, but she continued to stagger ahead.[2]

In Chihuahua we were put in prison. Men came to examine us as though they were purchasing horses. Siki was so weak that she was rejected. Big Water told a *rico* that I am a Medicine Woman and had dressed the officer's arm. I feared that he might take me, but he chose the woman beside me. Because of their weakened condition five others were not sold. In Mexican jails prisoners are not fed, but depend upon their friends to bring food. Big Water supplied our needs until we were placed upon a train and shipped to the City of Mexico.

More buyers inspected us in another prison. One man bought four, including Siki. When he started away with them she ran back and threw her arms around me. He nodded, and the jailer let me go with them. He mounted his horse, and with another rider herded us through the streets after dark. I knew by the stars that we were going north. As houses became widely spaced I could see that there were small fields of maguey on either side. He stopped at a gate, a large iron one, and unlocked it. We were taken into a big house, built much like a fort, and enclosing a central patio. Next morning we were given food and water, and permitted to bathe. A Mexican woman about my age took charge of us and set us to carrying wood, drawing water from the well, scrubbing walks, and doing other tasks much easier than those to which we were accustomed. Except for the captivity the life was not hard. I urged the younger women to obey cheerfully, and to be respectful to our owners. We all knew a few words of their language, and picked up more quickly.

Sometimes three were taken outside the house and put to work collecting the juice of the maguey used for a drink they call *pulque.* When the plant begins to throw up the stalk, the thorny leaves about the base are cut away with big knives, the blossom stalk cut off, and a hollow scooped out. The juice collects in this and is drawn from it into skin bags. The Mexicans say water causes sickness and this drink does not. That is true.

Stone walls separated one small patch of land from another. Three of the young women were taken from us and put in the adjoining field to work. I arranged signals for communication before their going. The overseer did not permit Siki and me to go near the wall. I was not in the field much, but was given tasks about the house. The children of the family liked me and I cared for their needs.

Each evening at sunset Siki came to me. I had to depend upon her to communicate with the others. I planned to escape, but did not wish to leave them. I knew that the *tunas* of the prickly pear ripen in that land in winter; at Ojo Caliente, in summer. I thought that if we could get away while those fruits were edible we might find ripe ones all along the way to the Río Grande.

Without blankets and knives we dared not attempt the trip. Each must have a blanket. At least one must secure a butcher knife. But how? In the kitchen the knives were carefully counted and locked up for the night. The machetes used in the field were too large for our purpose. The first winter passed with no possibility for escape. So did the next. Five came and went before I dared make the attempt.

By that time I was a trusted servant, permitted to do the daily marketing. One morning at the *mercado* I passed a meat stall and heard a cry of *Ladron!* People left their merchandise to chase the boy. While the butcher was watching the pursuit I slipped a long, keen knife under my skirt. Day and night I kept it concealed in my clothing.

At last the *tunas* ripened. I sought an opportunity to get word to the three on the other side of the wall that the time was at hand. I got permission to let the children walk in the field. As we strolled along we picked up small stones. The boy threw them at birds. I slipped five into the top of my *reboso*. As I leaned against the wall I placed five on top of the wall, with the largest to the north. Around each I had wrapped a leaf. I placed under them a cactus fiber with three knots in it. I knew that if Huera found my sign that she would interpret it to mean that all five were to have blankets and leave in three days. Not until sunset of the appointed day did I tell Siki my plans. I was sent on an errand to the overseer. He went to the house in response to my message, and Siki and I climbed the wall. We joined the women strolling toward the small church outside the gate. As we passed the next field, Huera and the others joined us. I sent Siki and two others across the street and strolled leisurely along with Huera. We were dressed as were the *peons,* and nobody noticed us. The gates of the city were kept open until those who attended vesper services returned. We were not stopped, but walked beside a man and his wife to the door of the church. There I stopped to fasten the thong of my *huaraches,* and saw the others across the road. I walked on past the church, and still there were no pursuers.

It was a very dark night. When we heard vehicles or horses we left the road and hid until they had passed. All that night we walked, but toward morning I began looking for a hiding place. There was little brush, few big stones. We heard the noise of shod hoofs approaching and crawled under a low bridge. Light was breaking as hoofs thundered overhead. All that day we crouched behind the arches with no food, no water. *Carretas,* coaches, horsemen, and pedestrians passed over the bridge. Had a child wandered down the slope or a dog scented us we would have been returned to the city. With the welcome darkness came fewer travelers and we left our hiding place to walk parallel with the road. It was almost morning before we passed a *jacal* with no dog on guard. Siki cut a water jug from a beam above the door, and we filled it from the little trickle of water we found nearby. Then we hid in some brush and ate *tunas*. Nobody stayed on guard while we slept, for we were exhausted, and had we been discovered could have had no chance to get away.

I think we had been walking for about a week when we found a water hole about which were the tracks of cattle. We lay hidden hoping to catch and kill a calf. If we got one its mother would attack us; and we had to wait until three of about a year old each came to drink. We cut one's throat, and skinned it. We cut off the meat and wrapped it in blankets. We took the stomach for a water bag. Then we tried to obliterate tracks because it was probable that a *vaquero* would water his horse and learn of our presence. Buzzards would take care of the rest.

Again we hid to slice and dry the meat, and to make foot-coverings, for our *huaraches* were badly worn. During the light of the moon we moved cautiously, avoiding villages, and constantly watching for riders. At times we separated, each taking a different route to reassemble at some conspicuous landmark to our north.

Only Huera had brought a blanket. She had wrapped it about her body under her full skirt. The nights were cold, and our covering through the day insufficient. We longed for a fire but did not dare risk making one. I made fire sticks to be used when we thought it safe.

Not until we neared Chihuahua did I know where we were. I recognized the place by the contour of the mountains. We circled The City of Mules widely, and at a water hole we killed another calf. We gathered very dry wood and built a fire in a deep arroyo at midday. For the first time since leaving Mexico City we cooked food.

We had been on the way about three months, and our clothing was in tatters, and our feet bare. With fresh skin we wrapped our feet and struck out northwest in order to avoid El Paso del Norte and cross the Border south of the Florida Mountains. At Tres Hermanas we rested three days, and there we killed another beef. Then we headed for the cache in the Floridas in which Victorio had stored supplies six years before. We planned to rest there and make dresses of the calico taken from the smuggler's train. It was impossible to go to Monticello without more clothing than we had.

Twice I had visited that cave but had difficulty in approaching it from the south. When I saw the woods I looked for a spring, and knew that we were close to the cave. Unfortunately the bolts of cloth had been badly damaged by mice, but we salvaged what we could and made dresses. The best pieces we carried with us to exchange for food when we reached Monticello, the village on the Cañada Alamosa where our people had traded with the Mexicans.

We circled wide from Fort Cummings, and set out north. Then we crossed the low divide beyond the Canyon Cuchillo and went to the village. Up the river was our headquarters and home. If we found none of our people there we had only to wait, for they would come.

There was a new trader at Monticello and he did not know us. He thought we had stolen the cloth. We spoke Spanish fluently but he did not credit our story of having walked from Mexico City. He took us into the trading post, gave us food, and furnished blankets for us to sleep on the floor in the storeroom. But he would not let us leave the building. We told him we could walk to Fort Apache, where he said our people were, but he would not permit us to leave. He warned us of danger from the wild animals and the cavalry — as though we did not know!

The villagers identified us before the cavalry arrived.

They brought us here.[3]

The Outbreak

Though Tzoe was stationed at San Carlos he came frequently to Fort Apache, presumably as messenger. There was a telegraph line between the places, and we wondered why it was necessary to send a man to deliver orders. Tzoe and Chato were very close friends, and both were heartily disliked and distrusted by our people. They were responsible for rumors that Kaytennae had been killed, and that Geronimo, Nana, and Chihuahua were to be imprisoned or killed. They and Mickey Free kept the Chiricahua and Warm Springs expecting trouble all the time.

Nana reminded both that not one of the three had been loyal to his own people—if Mickey *had* any people—and that, inevitably, all would betray the White Eyes as they had us. They were not to be believed under any circumstances, and it was probably not true that Kaytennae was dead. It was not true, either, that the chiefs were to have their heads chopped off as Chato was continually indicating. Our men knew, though, that as first sergeant, Chato had power over the scouts under him; and that some of them really liked him — especially Coonie and Martine. He was in a position to cause us much trouble, even as he had Kaytennae.

Except for the dread of betrayal our people were in good condition. They had raised crops, and harvested wild food. They had killed deer and dried venison, and they had tanned skins for clothing

[175]

and for covering arbors. They had ground both acorn and corn meal. They had corn not only for bread but for *tiswin,* of which they were very fond. Huera, a woman who had married Chihuahua, was expert in its manufacture. Though it was unfermented and mild, quantities of it produced intoxication. A drunken man was arrested and imprisoned for beating his wife. That was the charge. When Lieutenant Davis questioned him he made no defense. That confirmed the Apaches in their suspicion that his wife had been unfaithful to him. Of course no man would admit such a thing about his wife. Our people left the punishment of the guilty woman to the discretion of the husband. The usual punishment was death or cutting off her nose. I have seen a few old women so disfigured. I have heard of infidelity being punished by burning both the guilty man and woman, but I have never seen either done. Consequently, if Gar's wife got off with a beating he was being lenient.

Even before the days of distillates Apaches drank more than they should. Liquor has been responsible for hundreds of deaths. But when they made the pact with General Crook no promises were given, either as to what they should drink or how they should discipline their families. They had scrupulously kept the promises they made, but upon these subjects they had not committed themselves. The young officer undertook to put a stop to both wife-beating and intoxication.[1] Our people definitely recognized each as a vice, but not one over which the lieutenant had jurisdiction.[2] He was delegating undue authority to himself and the scouts when he undertook to meddle with private lives. Even Loco supported Chihuahua in his opposition to interference in domestic affairs.

Loco was on very good terms with the officer and he undertook to state Chihuahua's case. Chihuahua had been drinking and was impatient with the long harangue, and especially with Mickey Free's distorting and twisting his replies to Davis. When the officer began lecturing the chiefs against indulgence in a habit they knew he shared, Chihuahua stood and indignantly stalked from the meeting. Nana, whose disgust was occasioned by the interpreter rather than the lieutenant, issued an order to Mickey: "Tell the Fat Boy that I had killed many men before he was out of baby grass." He left followed by every other leader except Loco.

The chiefs and head men went immediately into council because they anticipated wholesale arrests. They had broken no promises. But neither had Kaytennae. And what had been done to him? Chato could not be believed, but there was a possibility that he had spoken the truth about Father's death.

The report he had given about Captain Crawford no longer being at San Carlos might be true. If he had asked for a transfer and been replaced by a new man who knew little of Apaches there was no telling what he might do to gain promotion. Though they liked Britton Davis they did not hesitate to let him know that they would not submit to restrictions to which they had not agreed. He realized the seriousness of the situation, though not the instigators of it, and notified the new commander at San Carlos.[3] Had General Crook received that message he could undoubtedly have averted the break from the reservation. But it was not relayed to him. Meanwhile Davis had told Nana that Nantan Lupan was to decide upon subsequent methods of handling the situation. He insisted that no order had come. To them that indicated serious possibilities.

On May 17, 1885, about a hundred forty people, of whom thirty-seven were men, left the reservation.[4] Nana would not permit either Mother or Grandmother to go. Siki had married Toklanni and remained with her husband. Nana rode with them. Mangus was detailed to command the guard in charge of the women and children. He took Daklugie, son of Juh, and Istee, son of Victorio. Geronimo, Naiche, and their warriors comprised the rear guard. They hoped that their absence would escape notice till morning, but took the precaution of cutting the telegraph wires to San Carlos. In the past the wire had been cut and miles of it thrown into deep canyons. Men had gone out with new wire and repaired the lines. Geronimo was determined that word should not reach the cavalry at San Carlos, but was at a loss to prevent it. Grandfather sent the boys up the trees to cut the wire, tie the ends to limbs with buckskin thongs, and conceal the breaks. They did this in many places — wherever they found the wire attached to a tree. His method was effective. But their absence was discovered and reported to Davis by Mickey Free. To divert suspicion both Chapo and Perico had been left with the officer, but were to slip away and overtake us as soon as Davis knew we were gone. This they did.

The band rode hard, picking up horses as they went, changing mounts frequently, and making no stops except to cut wires. They were about twenty miles in advance of the cavalry when from the top of a ridge they sighted dust. They learned later that the pursuers turned back. In the Mogollons they separated into small groups, each of which took a different route. Mangus rode straight for Mexico with his family and the two boys he had taken into his family. His was the smallest of the groups.

Chihuahua turned north. That night he camped on a ridge with an almost perpendicular cliff at his back and a steep slope on either side. On the east the canyon was narrow enough for danger of firing from the opposite slope, but he did not anticipate that it might come soon. He killed a beef for his hungry band, and they left pieces roasting for the morning meal. He concealed the horses in a valley to the west and all were informed as to procedure in case of surprise.

Eugene and Ramona Chihuahua have told me of that occurrence. Eugene was ten or eleven years old. He and another lad took bows and arrows to hunt squirrels while breakfast was being prepared. Strolling along the ridge they noticed a very steep, slick place, almost perpendicular, over which water fell in rainy weather. Suddenly a bullet whistled past them. They thought one of the men had shot at a deer until Eugene's companion fell with blood streaming from his arm. He was unable to lift the boy to his feet.

"Run! Save yourself!" urged the lad.

Eugene tried to drag the child to cover. His aunt ran to him, lifted the wounded one to her shoulder, and hurried to the dry bed of the waterfall. A man overtook her and relieved her of her burden. Many shots were fired, and bullets were thick about them.

"Slide down!" he ordered.

Eugene looked, and far below saw his uncle standing with arms held for him. The slide was smooth, but very steep. He shrank from it till his aunt grabbed his shoulders and pushed him over, feet first. He closed his eyes, and felt hands catch and ease him to the earth. The wounded lad followed, and then the aunt. Her weight toppled the man to earth and when he had regained his footing the man slid against him.

While men raced for horses, women took refuge in a cave. Warriors tried to decoy the cavalry into pursuing them in order to enable the helpless to escape, but were unsuccessful. Several people were killed; several were wounded. A woman shot through the leg mounted a horse and rode with the other captives. She suffered greatly from loss of blood and had to be carried to the jail at the fort [Bowie]. There a doctor dressed the boy's arm, but the woman got no help. The children were permitted to play outside the building in which the women were held. The men were in another place.

Eugene's mother sent him for prickly pear leaves for dressing the woman's leg. It was healing until all the women were put to work digging a ditch for a latrine. The crippled one struggled to work with the rest. When she fell, the others found a stick which they bound to her leg with strips of a blanket. She tried to return to the jail and a soldier knocked her down with his rifle. He beat her until she never got up again. With bowed heads the women labored at the ditch until they were marched back to the building.

The next morning her body was gone.[5]

Meanwhile, Chihuahua had ridden hard for the border. He surprised a small force, killed two troopers, wounded several, and captured both ammunition and fresh horses. What he could not carry he burned. The cavalry that chased him reported that he had stopped only to change mounts and had covered ninety miles before permitting his band to stop. There were women and children with his men. Along the route of that wild flight they found the bodies of two new-born infants.

They followed Chihuahua into Mexico and to the foothills of the Sierra Madre. Captain Crawford knew Apaches and their ways. He knew that they could not be overtaken with heavy equipment impeding the movements of the cavalry. Though his scouts could trail Chihuahua the cavalry could not. They had captured the women and children sent to Fort Bowie, but the warriors were vastly superior to them in covering distance. Crawford depended entirely upon his scouts for fighting. If the cavalry were to keep near them they must abandon the heavy loads on the ammunition mules, and substitute burros with light ones.

Chihuahua was almost out of ammunition. He sent his brother, Ulzanna (Josannie) on a raid for it. With a few picked men Ulzanna dashed across the border where there were about eighty troops in the field. Though the Nantan Lupan* had stationed guards at the water holes and dangerous crossings, Ulzanna succeeded in his mission. He returned with two hundred fifty horses, and a train of ammunition mules. He had ridden hundreds of miles, killed only those who opposed him, and returned without the loss of a man.

---

*The Apache name for General Crook.

Ulzanna, like the rest, knew that the hordes of the enemy could not be combated forever. The odds were too great, the result inevitable. Nana had three men; Geronimo, twenty; Chihuahua, about the same number. Though they were fighting men such as the world had never before produced they could not compete with thousands of soldiers well equipped and well supplied with ammunition. Yet they did not consider giving up the unequal struggle. They determined to be free so long as one man remained, unconquered, unconquerable.

Since Tres Castillos our people had known the outcome. Nana knew well how the struggle would end. His little band had fled so often, starved so much, slept so little, and suffered so long that death had no terrors. For that matter it never has terrorized Apaches as it seems to White Eyes. They have too much faith in Ussen to fear what is in store for them in The Happy Place. Leaving their families and friends is bad, yes; the suffering that sometimes precedes death is to be dreaded. But the life beyond — it is much better than that on this earth.

Lieutenant Davis, with Chato in charge of the scouts, followed to Mexico. In Chihuahua they lost both horses and supplies. They turned northeast and walked to the ranch of a *rico* near the Mexican border. He fed them, but did not give them mounts. They followed the trail to the railroad and walked up the tracks to El Paso del Norte, from which place they crossed into Texas.

Not long after this, Britton Davis resigned his commission and became manager of Los Corralitos, a big ranch in Chihuahua. My people have wondered if his leaving the service were not because of his feeling that the government had treated us unjustly, or if he had not learned that he had been deceived by his trusted interpreter and scout.

Years later, Frank Lockwood visited the Mescalero Reservation. There he interviewed Eugene Chihuahua, his sister, Ramona Chihuahua, Daklugie, and several other old Chiricahuas who had been released from the twenty-seven-years' servitude as prisoners of war. It is not the custom of my people to express their criticism of each other to White Eyes. But Lockwood wrote a very significant statement: "The aura of hate still lingers about the grave of Chato."

Surrender

Chihuahua overtook Geronimo in a canyon of the Sierra Madre. The west side is cut by deep *barrancas* with such steep slopes that the heights are difficult of access, and almost impassable except on foot. There Chapo and Perico joined them. If there had ever been hard feeling between Geronimo and Naiche it had been forgotten in the bond of the danger confronting them. Naiche was a superb fighting man.

Nana always maintained that the combined forces never exceeded thirty-five warriors. The young officers say thirty-seven, but under our loose organization it is difficult to estimate, for men came and went, as scouts and as messengers. Either number was infinitesimal in comparison to the hordes of cavalrymen and Tarahumaras that the U.S. and Mexico used harassing the Apaches. General Crook put eighty companies of infantry and cavalry in the field. But it was the scouts whom the Apaches dreaded, for only they knew the trails and the hiding places. And only they could traverse the country rapidly enough to be a menace. They got close enough to capture many of the horses and nearly all of the supplies. I think that only those men could have taken the risks necessary to partially replace what they had lost. Geronimo told me at Fort Sill that Grandfather planned and led the raids for ammunition.

There came a time when the Warm Springs Apaches were so reduced in numbers and equipment that Geronimo permitted Lozen to go to Captain Crawford and arrange for a meeting. There were some among them who wished to return to Turkey Creek, and Nana thought that all the women and children should. Lozen took another woman, Dahteste, with her and reached the camp safely. The scouts recognized them; the officers promised safe conduct for Geronimo if he should come under a flag of truce.

The next morning a troop of Mexicans and Tarahumaras sighted the scouts and thought them to be Geronimo's band. Crawford sprang to a large boulder in sight of both forces and called to the Mexicans that his force was American. Others joined in the attempt to prevent a battle. A bullet hit Crawford and he fell and struck his head on the boulder. Lozen witnessed the fall; so did Kanseah. Both thought the fatal injury that resulted was caused by his striking his head on the stone rather than the glancing bullet.[1] Several Mexicans were killed, many wounded.

Lieutenant Maus took command of the troops and met with Geronimo. It was decided that the entire band was to go back to Fort Apache, but not until word could be carried to the stragglers

Geronimo's camp in the Sierra Madre of Mexico. Hiding in rugged terrain, about a mile from the camp of General Crook, the Chiricahua leader and his men captured the General's horses and many of his supplies, trying desperately to postpone surrender.

Smithsonian Institution Photo

in the mountains. Among these was Mangus and his little group who had kept apart since going to Mexico.[2] Chihuahua, too, refused to come in because his family was imprisoned at Fort Bowie. Many women and children, weary of the warpath, or separated from the men of their families, took refuge with Chihuahua.

Some of Geronimo's men decided that they would not enter the United States but would return to the Sierra. Geronimo and Naiche turned back with their band. One of Naiche's wives got about a half-mile from the cavalry and decided to return to them. She ran toward the scouts, and to prevent other desertions Naiche fired at her. The bullet struck her in the leg. She was the mother of Dorothy, whom I later married.

Lieutenant Maus tried to induce Chihuahua to surrender. The chief replied that without proof of his family's being alive at Bowie he would not quit fighting. The young officer told him to select a man to go and see about his family. Chihuahua sent Perico as a hostage, and the scouts returned with Chihuahua's family. One child was not with them; and Maus sent to Fort Apache and had him brought to the others. The band was put aboard a train for Florida.

Nana had consented to go with Maus because he thought that there was still a chance to make peace and return to Turkey Creek if he could talk with General Crook. They soon learned that Crook had been replaced by General Miles — the Nantan Lupan was a stern and unyielding enemy, but one whose word to them was good. They knew nothing of the new commander except that he increased the number of troops stationed about the water holes and put heliographs into operation.

Captain H. W. Lawton, an officer trained under General Crook, operated in northern Mexico for about four months, and during that time captured ponies and food supplies. His troops could not keep up with the scouts; they could not stand the rains and other hardships of the pursuit over mountains and through canyons. Geronimo replenished his own supplies by cutting off horses and stealing ammunition from the troops. But Lieutenant Gatewood, in charge of the scouts, was a real menace. He had been brought from Fort Stanton because of his knowledge and experience with Apaches. With him were Martine and Kayitah whom Miles had recruited at Fort Apache because of their knowledge of the trails and haunts of Geronimo in Mexico. Martine and Kayitah were promised seventy thousand dollars if they succeeded in contacting Geronimo and inducing him to surrender.[3] That was a large sum of money, but a trifle in comparison to what the campaign was costing the government. Needless to say — they did not collect!

Geronimo's fighting force was very small. I knew every one of them: Naiche, Nana, Fun, Eyelash, Chapo, Yanosha, Kanseah, Zhunne, Ahnondia, Matzus, Bishi, Bihido, Lizah [Lozen], Hanlonah, Nahpeh and Perico. There may be those who question their judgment in prolonging a hopeless situation but I doubt that anyone who really knows conditions can question their resourcefulness and courage. Many people honor Cochise and Mangas Coloradas, but condemn Geronimo because he held out longer.

Martine was a Nednhi and at times had been on raids with Geronimo. He knew that some of the men were tired of the warpath, and that the women and children were exhausted. Nineteen helpless people — one should except Lozen — with fewer men than the scouts themselves! Martine had relatives among them; so did Kayitah. General Miles relied upon these ties to induce the little band to cease fighting. It was suspected that Geronimo was camped on a flat-topped mountain in a bend of the Bavispe River. There the band could live indefinitely even if the zigzag trail which was the only way to the top should be destroyed. There was one inducement that might prevent their choosing to isolate themselves from the world — some of the men's families were elsewhere. If they chose isolation they would never see their wives and children again.

Jasper Kanseah of Geronimo's band was on guard with field glasses when Martine and Kayitah were sighted, moving dots upon the trail. He says:

I was born on Cochise's Reservation and remember seeing our great chief. My father was killed before I was born and my mother before I can remember. With my grandmother I was driven to San Carlos. After she died, the other women gave me food and cared for me as their own. I had no relative but Geronimo. He took me to be trained as a warrior when I could not have been more than thirteen. Yanosha, one of the bravest, was my sponsor.

At the time of the surrender I was still very young, though I had long been a warrior. I lay at the head of the trail with field glasses. When I detected a movement on the plain far below I watched carefully. Something very small was crossing the plain; no — two things. Might be deer. They got a little bigger; not long enough for deer. I called to Geronimo that somebody was coming. He knew that it would take half a day for anyone to climb the trail and told me to keep watch and when I was sure it was men to report. I was already sure, but waited a while to say so. He sent another guard to stay with me. As the figures toiled up the trail I recognized Martine and Kayitah. Our warriors joined us and seated themselves with Yanosha at Geronimo's right, and Fun, Eyelash, and Zhunne at his left. The scouts came on, Martine carrying a stick with a white rag tied to it. I could distinguish their faces, and I told Geronimo who they were.

"It does not matter who they are. If they come closer they are to be shot."

"They are our brothers," said Yanosha, "Let's find why they come. They are brave men to risk this."

"They do not take the risk for us, but for the money promised by the White Eyes. When they get close enough, shoot!"

"We will not shoot," said Yanosha. "If there is any more fighting done it will be with you, not them. The first man who lifts a rifle I will kill."

"I will help you," said Fun.

Among the Apaches who became Scouts for the American military were several major figures in Kaywaykla's story. The Chiricahua Naiche, son of Cochise, is third from the left in the second row. To the left of Naiche is Perico, and to the right, Johnny Loco.

Geronimo knew they made no threats they did not intend to fulfill. He knew that either man would kill him, for neither could be intimidated.

"Let them come," he grunted.

They were within rifle range. When they got close enough to hear, Yanosha cried, "Come up! Nobody is going to hurt you."

They reminded Geronimo of his plight and of the uselessness of further fighting. They told him that Chihuahua with his band and some of the wives and children of the men beside Geronimo were already in Florida. They reminded him that every living thing — Mexicans, Americans, and even the beasts — were his enemies. The mountain itself was both a shield and a menace, for if the trail were destroyed he was forever a prisoner upon it.

"How do we know that Gatewood will keep his promise to take us to our families?" he asked.

"He has given his word. He will take you first to Fort Bowie, and there he will put you on the train to go to your families in Florida. In three days, five at most, you will be with them."

"You know well how many Apaches have been taken under safe conduct and been murdered. And think what happened to Kaytennae!"

Geronimo knew of Kaytennae's return. He had come first to San Carlos, and had accompanied General Crook to the Cañon de los Embudos. During the historic conference Kaytennae had sat beside Nana, as next in rank.

Kanseah went on: Geronimo said, "This is my home. Here I stay. Kill me if you wish, for every living thing has to die sometime. How can a man meet death better than in fighting for his own?"

"But your men do not have their families with them as you do. If you do not quit fighting soon there will be none of you left. The Chiricahua will be exterminated."

"I prefer death to imprisonment."

"You will not be imprisoned. Lieutenant Gatewood has said so. He asks only that you meet him in council."

"Mangas Coloradas trusted to the white flag. What happened to him?"

"Gatewood will keep his word. Think of the women and children with you — your own wives and children among them."

Geronimo agreed to talk with the young officer and met him

Nana, venerable chief of the Warm Springs and great-uncle of the narrator, is the center figure in this picture of Apache leaders. To the left of Nana are Geronimo and Chihuahua, and to his right Chief Loco and Ulzana.

on a spot of the Apache's selection. A few at a time, the warriors went in, each retaining his weapons. The interpreters they distrusted were not present; neither was Chato. Geronimo's Mescalero wife and her daughter accompanied him and Chapo. Dahteste was with Lozen.

Nana opposed the surrender. Naiche, warworn and discouraged, seemed indifferent. The warriors whose families were with them supported Nana. It was the lure of being reunited with their wives and children that turned the tide of opinion among the others. Geronimo demanded that if his men gave up they should be returned to Turkey Creek and reinstated on their reservation. Gatewood promised that they would not be killed, but warned them that they would not be returned to Fort Apache in their former status. And Gatewood told Geronimo that if he were an Apache he would surrender to General Miles who could be depended upon to keep his word.[4]

General Miles! The Apaches did not know him. They trusted Crook; whether they could trust his successor they doubted. The Apaches decided to sleep on it. The next morning they agreed to go to Bowie with Gatewood. It was decided that Captain Lawton and his command should travel with them, but that Gatewood remain among them and sleep in their camp. In September, 1886, the warriors met General Miles near the Border and agreed to go to Florida on condition of being immediately reunited with their families.

The claim that General Miles, Captain Lawton, or anybody else — Agent Clum included — ever captured Geronimo is false. Of that there is proof. Yet Miles and Lawton unhesitatingly took credit for doing so; they were feted in Tucson, and apparently thought that the true account of the surrender would never be made known to the public. They thought they had nothing to fear from the inarticulate Apaches who were present.[5]

General Miles

Grandfather was very angry because General Miles considered him too old and infirm to be a source of danger. With five others he went to the mountains and there he waged a war of his own until it suited him to return to Turkey Creek. When Kaytennae made us a brief visit he met Nana at our arbor. He knew that Grandfather questioned his being with the scouts, and explained that in the years of imprisonment at Alcatraz he had learned that he could best serve his people by doing so. He had learned to speak English fairly well but not to read and write. He could see to it that the interpreters did not twist the meaning of the messages they conveyed to the cavalry. He could check on the scouts. He urged Grandfather to stay at Fort Apache with us and see that the non-combatants remained there, free of molestation.

Nana shook his head, but he stayed.

Mangus had with him two warriors, their wives, three small children, his son (Frank Mangus), Istee, and Daklugie. A month after Geronimo surrendered, these Apaches came through the Rancho Corralitos of which Britton Davis had become manager, and drove off some mules, perhaps fifty. General Miles was informed, and his men secured and returned most of the animals. They reported also that they had captured Mangus, but the testimony of Mangus and his party was that they had voluntarily given

[190]

up. Daklugie spoke Spanish well, and in the absence of an officer, Mangus sent Daklugie to the camp where he found only a few guards and the cook. He stated that his mission was surrender, and upon the return of the officer, who was Captain Charles Cooper of the Tenth Infantry, Mangus' party went in and were sent to Fort Apache.[1]

Then occurred one of those actions that completely bewildered the Apaches except as a confirmation of their distrust in General Miles: the scouts were rounded up with the hostiles and forced to share their imprisonment. Many had served the cavalry faithfully and incurred the contempt of their own people to aid the White Eyes. And for this they were made prisoners of war for twenty-seven years! To Geronimo and his band this justified their sense of vengeance and was the silver lining in the dark cloud that enveloped them.

It was with mixed emotions that we Apaches at Turkey Creek received the news. If the scouts had been made prisoners of war, what was in store for us? True, we were noncombatants, but though we had come in voluntarily we also might be taken to Florida. Orders for each person — rather than the head of the family, as was the custom — to report to Fort Apache for rations, increased our uneasiness. We knew that Kaytennae would let us know what to expect if he were able, but it was quite possible that he had been shipped to Florida.

General Ely S. Parker, after his retirement, wrote an article regarding Miles' so-called capture of Geronimo, and the disposition of the Chiricahua at Fort Apache.[2]

Parker said:

Early in June, 1886, General Miles arrived at Fort Huachuca. To get an idea of the country he and I climbed to the summit of El Moro Mountain near the post. I have never been slow at suggestions and I took this opportunity to ask General Miles if I might make one.

"I have recently come from Fort Apache where the Chiricahua not with Geronimo were located," I said. "Whenever there is news of a raid, the Chiricahua, in order not to be involved in the fighting, go into the post and are quartered in the quartermaster's corral."

"I would suggest that a false report of a raid be spread, and when the Indians are in the corral, that they be surrounded by the troops, disarmed, taken to the railroad and shipped east as prisoners of war. Geronimo's band in the field will then be isolated, will no longer receive aid and comfort, as heretofore, and will surrender."

"Why, that would be treachery," said the General. "I could never do that."

General Miles had pronounced the judgment in which all Apaches concur. Again, let Miles' own words bear witness to his actions:

It will be remembered that one class or race is without representation, and has not the advantages of the press or telegraph to bring it into communication with the intelligence of the world, and that it has seldom been heard except in the cry of alarm and conflict along the Western Frontier.

Could we but perceive the true character of the Indians, and learn what their dispositions are when not covered by the cloak of necessity, policy, and interest, we should find that they have always regarded us as a body of false and cruel invaders of their country, while we in turn are too apt to consider them as a treacherous and bloodthirsty race who should be destroyed by any or all means. . . . It is unfair to suppose that one party has invariably acted rightly and that the other is responsible for every wrong that has ever been committed . . . . In our treaty relationships, most extravagant and yet sacred promises have been given by the highest authorities, and these have been frequently disregarded. . . .

Coming down to our direct or immediate relations with them, we find that our policy has been to make them wards of the nation, to be held under close military surveillance, or else to make them pensioners under no other restraint than the influence of one or two individuals. Living under the government, yet without any legitimate government, without any law and without any physical power to control them, what better subjects or more propitious fields could be found for vice and crime?

We have committed our Indian matters to the custody of an Indian Bureau which for many years was a part of the military establishment of the government; but for political reasons, and to promote party interest, this bureau was transferred to the Department of Interior.

Whether or not our system of Indian management has been

a success during the past ten, fifty, or one hundred years, is almost answered in the asking. The Indians, the frontiersmen, the army stationed in the West, and the readers of the daily news in all parts of our country, can answer that question.

The Chiricahuas were the worst, wildest, and strongest of all. The Apache regarded himself as the first man, the "superior man," as the word Apache [Tinne] indicates. In some respects they really were superior. They excelled in strength, activity, endurance, and also in cruelty.

•   •   •

Yet this man — General Miles — who did have an unusual understanding of our problem, and who condemned as treachery the suggestion of corralling my people and shipping them to Florida, did exactly that. He did it, furthermore, by remote control.

I was about nine when we went to Fort Apache to avoid being suspected of aiding the hostiles. I remember well the terror of the noncombatants as we huddled together to avoid suspicion. Unarmed and entirely blameless, we awaited the verdict that would permit our return to our camps. Instead of that verdict, came the order from General Miles to take us prisoners.

Again I quote Miles:

I went to the telegraph office and asked the operator on duty, a bright and intelligent young man, if he would not open communication with the operator at Fort Apache, and *in his own name, without mentioning my presence* [author's italics] ask for the news of what was going on. He did so, and the operator at Fort Apache, whose office occupied a high point so that he could overlook the whole scene from his window, replied that he observed that all the Indians had been gathered in to be counted according to the custom on Sundays. Also as was their usual practice, the troops had gone through their Sunday inspection, and after they had performed their ordinary duties, had taken certain positions that commanded the position of the Indians.

All this merely served to increase my anxiety while I was awaiting results. Then this operator at Willcox said to the other one at Fort Apache, two hundred miles distant:

"Let me know fully what is going on."

And he replied, "I will."

He saw the troops suddenly take positions surrounding the large body of Indians, and absolutely commanding the position of the Indian camp. He saw some commotion among the Indians. All the warriors took a standing position ready for immediate action. He saw Colonel Wade quietly walk down to their vicinity and command them all to sit down. The Indians, realizing the folly of resistance in the presence of this strong body of troops, and that there was no avenue of escape for them, were entirely within the control of the troops and quietly obeyed the command of Colonel Wade. All this was flashed over the wires to the operator at Willcox, who as little realized the importance of it as did the operator who sent the message.

I waited for another dispatch which said that Colonel Wade had commanded the warriors to leave the camp and to go into one of the large buildings adjacent to the body of troops. A fourth dispatch stated that Colonel Wade had directed a number of women to return to their camps and bring in their goods and all that they required to carry them, as they were to be removed.

•   •   •

Grandmother and I waited with the men while Mother and Siki went for our belongings. They tied what they could in blankets and skins and brought the things to the corral.

We were sent by wagons, under cavalry escort, to Holbrook, Arizona. There we were herded aboard the train and shipped to Florida — about four hundred people who had kept their promises, and who had every right to expect the government of the United States to do the same.

$\mathcal{F}$lorida

It was our train, and not the one which took Geronimo's band to Florida, from which Massai escaped.[1] He had not been in the car with Mother and me, but word of his jumping from the train came to us. He had waited long for the engine to climb a grade, for he knew that when it did it must slow down. Day after day the train went downhill; then it moved across level land, but finally Massai could tell that the engine was laboring up a slope. It was somewhere in Missouri that Massai broke the window in the coach and he and Gray Lizard jumped from the train. Lizard was a Tonkawa who had wandered west and had long been with Massai. Since the government was concerned only with the Apaches, no official report of the Tonkawa's escape was made. The two men hid by day and traveled by night until they reached the Mescalero Reservation, and that without being seen by white people.

We crossed the Mississippi at St. Louis, and were taken from the train at St. Augustine, Florida. There we were placed in a walled fort where we cooked the food issued to us. I have been told that it was the old Spanish fort. Some Catholic Sisters undertook to teach the children a little English, and provided baths, clothing, and sometimes medicine. They tried to teach us to conform to civilized standards of living. I will never forget the kindness of those good women, nor the respect in which we held them. For the first time in my life

One of the Southern Pacific trains carrying Apache prisoners to Florida in 1886 stopped near the Nueces River in Texas. The Warm Springs Medicine Woman, Lozen, is in the picture, third from the right in the top row. Geronimo is third from the right below, and reading toward the left are Naiche, son of Cochise, and Perico and Fun, half-brothers to Geronimo.

I saw the interior of a church and dimly sensed that the White Eyes, too, worshipped Ussen. I realized more fully that not all White Eyes were cruel and ruthless, but that there were some among them who were gentle and kind.

I will not forget, either, the first death from natural causes among us. I had seen hundreds of people killed, but though I knew that old people sometimes died because of their years, I had not realized that it could happen to the young. A girl passed away, my people said, from heartbreak and loneliness. Men took her body away in a box — a terrible thing to us. Whether she was buried, we had no way of knowing. That to us was much worse than death caused by violence; and it was the first of many, many, that were to follow. Ours were a mountain people, and moreover, a dry land people. We were accustomed to dry heat, but in Florida the dampness and the mosquitoes took toll of us until it seemed that none would be left. Perhaps we were taken to Florida for that purpose; from our point of view shooting would have been much less cruel.

The promise to put the men with their families was, of course, not kept. Nor were the men informed as to the location of their families. Neither group knew whether the other was living. Geronimo bitterly regretted having surrendered. In later years he said repeatedly that he should have stayed in his homeland though nobody but Nana remained there to die with him.

The Apaches had one consolation in a loyal friend who had come from San Carlos to interpret for them. George Wratten had grown up in the trader's store on the reservation at San Carlos and spoke Apache fluently. He was sympathetic and understanding with the Indians, and helped them in every way he could. He not only stayed with them in Florida, but accompanied them to Alabama, and eventually to Fort Sill, Oklahoma.

Mr. Wratten was aboard the train that carried Geronimo and his men east. At San Antonio the band was taken off the cars and housed in tents under guard. Mr. Wratten interpreted for them, attempted to learn the cause of the delay, and to assure them that they were not to be killed. He told them that the officers had written to Washington for orders.

"To kill us?" inquired Geronimo.

"I do not think so; but I do not know."

Wratten had a tent with them, and was permitted to keep

Geronimo, though he was never a chief, became legendary as leader of the last band of Apache to surrender to American military power before 27 years of custody, first in Florida, then in Fort Sill, Oklahoma. The humid Southeast was devastating to the Southwestern desert and mountain dwellers, many of whom died. Geronimo lived to regret his surrender and his confidence in General Miles.

weapons. Surreptitiously he added ammunition and rifles enough to equip several men. He told Geronimo that if an attempt were made to kill them that they need not be shot down unarmed. They were to get weapons from his tent.

"Ussen has said that I am not to be killed in battle, but am to live to be old. Long ago He told the Medicine Man so. Many times I have been wounded but I live. I am not to be killed. You will see."

"I hope that you are right." Wratten said. "But Ussen has not promised such for your men. It is not a bad idea to have access to weapons."

"Enjuh!"[2]

It seemed that neither the President nor the Secretary of War would admit the responsibility of the decision to send the Apaches to Florida. General Miles charged that he had sent a telegram stating that if he did not receive instructions to the contrary he would send them; that he had no reply; and that consequently he took the responsibility of arranging for their transportation. With everybody in authority offering alibis, and nobody being held responsible, Geronimo's band was held at San Antonio for a decision as to their destination. After about five weeks they were sent to Pensacola. Even George Wratten believed that they would be killed and reports made that they had tried to escape.

There was an investigation as to the number of deaths, and also as to the violation of the promise to unite the families. Public indignation was so great that Herbert Welsh, Secretary of the Indian Rights' Association, protested. Finally Washington authorized the two groups of Apaches to be united. They were happier, but the death rate remained high because of climatic conditions and malaria.

Again I saw Mangus and his band. Daklugie was not very old but he was six feet tall, and his hair hung to his knees. Istee was a young man, and Frank Mangus almost so. We were very happy until a new menace occurred. Officers and their wives went through the camp and selected over a hundred children to go to Pennsylvania to school. Part of them went by train, part by sea. I was with the latter, and I was the youngest child to go.[3] We were under the care of an officer and his wife; and except for the terror of another separation from our people, and the uncertainty of what was to be done with us, we were well treated. Being out of sight of land frightened us, but not more than the bewildering experience of crossing New York City.

At Carlisle we were subjected to the indignity of having our hair cut and being forced into trousers. Our clothes were sent to our families in Florida so that they might know that we still lived. How that could have convinced them I do not know but that is what we were told.

Both Kanseah and Chapo were among the students, possibly because they were both young and small. Jason, too, went, and he was a mature man. Again we encountered climatic conditions new to us and fatal to many. Chapo became tubercular, and was returned to his people to die.[4] Kanseah was unhappy and not interested in school. Captain Pratt let him return to his people after a few months. Daklugie made rapid progress in school; and I think I may say without boasting that I did. The Apache children learned to communicate with Indians of many other tribes who were in school; and eventually some of us learned the sign language which our people had never used. We learned English, too, both in school and in the homes in which we were placed to work during the summer.

My people have been said to be lacking in sense of humor, but that is a matter of opinion, as the few white people who have really known us would agree. Among our tragic experiences, one impressed us as very funny: The government gave Chato a medal and sent him to jail. From our point of view that was fully in accord with the inconsistencies of White Eyes, and the imprisonment justly deserved by Chato. He, Loco, Mickey Free, Coonie, Kaytennae, and others were promised in Washington, D.C. that because of services to the cavalry they were to be returned to Fort Apache. They were not. They were sent back to Florida instead.

White Eyes may have had delusions as to the purpose of Kaytennae in joining the scouts, but the Apaches did not. Kaytennae went along to see that the interpreters were honest and that Chato was held in check. When I think how uncomfortable Chato must have been with my father at his elbow, I know that Kaytennae had his revenge for the treachery that had sent him to prison. Losing face is a serious thing to the Apache, and Chato undoubtedly got his fill of it.

After they went to Washington and Chato was decorated with

The narrator, James Kaywaykla, was the youngest of more than a hundred Apache children separated from their parents in Florida and sent to Carlisle Indian School in Pennsylvania. Kaywaykla was nine years old when he was sent to school.

the big round medal that he always wore thereafter for photographs, they were put aboard a train and started west. When they reached Kansas they were taken off and imprisoned at Leavenworth. Again they were mystified, but no explanation was given. After a short time they were returned to Florida.[5] There was just no accounting for White Eyes' standards of justice. Regardless of the disappointment of the others, Kaytennae was happy to be with us again.

After spending eleven years at Carlisle I rejoined my people who had been taken to Fort Sill. They were living upon land generously given them by their brothers, the Kiowas, Comanches, and Kiowa-Apaches. They occupied this land until it was needed by the Army for an artillery range.

My people wanted very much to return to the Southwest. The Governor of Arizona said that if a train carrying them reached the border of Arizona Territory it would be dynamited; that Apaches were as dangerous as the rattlesnakes upon which they fed. Of course no Apache ever ate the flesh of any snake. No White Eye seems to understand the nature of our taboo against them, nor the antipathy of my people toward snakes. Today I do not know of one who would wear a belt or carry a billfold made from snakeskin.

• • •

Through the efforts of some of the younger men who had been given schooling at Carlisle (Asa Daklugie especially), the long-awaited release from bondage came. Added to their efforts were the death of Geronimo and the need of the military for the land we occupied. I was on the committee that inspected both the old reservation at Ojo Caliente and the one near the White Mountains in New Mexico.[6] The majority vote was for the latter. Also our people were given a choice: securing land around Lawton, Oklahoma, or going to the reservation. I have always been thankful that I chose the former. Those of us who settled on private land in Oklahoma encountered many difficulties, but I think are better off than those who are still in a sense prisoners, on the reservation.

For the latter are (in my opinion) still unfitted to take their places in modern economic society. This is above all an indictment of the system under which they have been compelled to exist. Until that system is improved, until a more intelligent effort is made to prepare Apaches to assume the citizenship they are supposed to have, they may become more despondent and more apathetic. I believe this to be the result of their hopelessness for the future of their children. Deprived of goals and incentive, present generations have lapsed into a condition as deplorable as it has been inescapable. A contemporary survey by psychologists indicated that the mixed breed of Mescalero, Chiricahua, Lipan, and Warm Springs on the Mescalero Reservation is lacking in initiative. Lacking in initiative! Yet these are the third and fourth generations of some of the bravest and most daring people of which the world has record!

My own grandchildren, through their mother, are descended from both Cochise and Mangas Coloradas. Not many women have been her superior, mentally, physically, or morally. Our children are from the lineage also of Victorio and Nana. Many more of the Chiricahua and Warm Springs children come from long lines of warriors and leaders — a group from which the unfit, the mentally slow, and the physically weak were eliminated by natural selection and war.

Why should such children lack initiative?

For eighty years now, the progenitors of these children have lived in situations in which decisions were made for them. Some of the decisions may have been wise, some not. The Apaches have exercised no initiative. Their lives have not been taken, they have not been confined in prisons. But they have lived in an economic and social prison that has had effects as bad or worse than a material one. They have owned little property individually, have made few decisions, and had little control over their destiny. Perhaps being dependent upon community property and bureaucratic decisions has had the effect on them that White Eyes fears from collective ownership or a totalitarian state for his own people.

Again — mine is an intensely religious people, and one with rigid standards of conduct. Today many of us have accepted the religion of White Eyes. To us Christianity is not just a beautiful legend to be used as an alibi or consolation for injustice, but a stern and just code of daily living — in this way comparable to our old religion. To those bound by neither, the transition stage is difficult. They are no longer inhibited by the old, or subject to the restrictions of the new. They have heard much of the brotherhood of man in

Christianity, but have seen little practice of it. They have heard much of Christian justice, but are not much impressed with the administration of it in their own affairs.

Before the night of oblivion closes in on my people, it is my prayer that something may be done to bring about change in their condition. I fear that improvement cannot be long delayed if the modern Apache is ever to stand upright and "face the Sun" — that is, stand up courageously to Life, as his fathers did. Diagnosing "the Apache problem" is a relatively simple matter. Anyone who lives near a reservation and has dealings with the people can do it. Finding new directions and helping people to follow them is another matter, not simple; but the need is great and immediate.

May the events of today and tomorrow begin to fulfill that need, and may the recollections of our children's children record the opening of new horizons and brighter days for the Apache people.

Notes to the Text

FLIGHT (pp. 1-10)

1. The Apaches called the Río Grande the "Great River," according to James Kaywaykla and others.
2. Grenville Goodwin, *Social Organization of the Western Apache*. Tucson: University of Arizona Press, 1968, or John C. Cremony, *Life Among the Apaches*. Reprint, Tucson: Arizona Silhouettes, 1954.

REFUGE (pp. 11-24)

1. Interview with Del Barton of El Paso, Texas, granddaughter of Grey Wolf, a chief of the Senecas.
2. Kaytennae, from *kah* (arrow) means "fight without arrows." The name was used by the Apaches to denote courage.
3. James Kaywaykla and Ace Daklugie, in interviews at the author's home in Ruidoso (1955), both stated that only "women who really loved their husbands went on the warpath with them." Lozen, while not married at that time, evidently had a special status commanding respect from the whole tribe. Therefore she must have been an exception to some of the restrictions concerning unmarried women.

THE MESCALERO RESERVATION (pp. 25-33)

1. Agent Godfroy's letter to the Commissioner of Indian Affairs at Mescalero.
2. Register.
3. Godfroy's letter. *Ibid.*
4. This statement about the origin of Loco's name was made to the author by Kaywaykla, Jasper Kanseah, Daklugie, and other Apache informants. It does not agree with information gained from other informants by historian Dan L. Thrapp.
5. Abel and Teodolo Chavez.
6. The runners were Nicholas and Kedizhinne.

[205]

7. Historical accounts conflict as to the removal of the Warm Springs people. Here the author records only the testimony of her informants.

8. Since the relationship between mosquitos and malaria was not actually announced until 1897, by Ronald Ross, a British pathologist, one assumes that Kaywaykla here was merging recollections of his people's understanding of illness with information he encountered later in life.

9. The Apaches interviewed by the author all regarded the white man as "superstitious about gold." To illustrate this they refer to the Gold Rush which caused invasion of the Apache domain in 1849, as well as to the regular stream of prospectors who came into Apache territory in search of gold. The Apaches did not appear to resent the trapper, nor later the rancher, as much as they did the prospector.

10. Interviews with Ace Daklugie and James Kaywaykla.

CEREMONIALS (pp. 35-44)

1. Interviews in Ruidoso with Paul Blazer, grandson of Dr. Joseph C. Blazer.

2. Godfroy letters. *Op Cit.*

3. According to Kaywaykla, red signified war to the Apaches.

HISTORY FROM OUR ANGLE (pp. 45-53)

1. The author has found records of copper ore being sent to Chihuahua only, but Kaywaykla insisted that ore was sometimes shipped to Durango as well.

2. James Kaywaykla, Ace Daklugie, and Eugene Chihuahua all agreed in the telling of this account which is somewhat in conflict with other reports.

3. In spite of Kaywaykla's assertion, neither Daklugie nor Chihuahua denied having seen scalps taken. However, each said it happened rarely, and usually only one was taken, to celebrate a war dance.

4. Cremony. *Op Cit.* His account differed materially from that of the author's Apache informants. For example, he reported 63 warriors killed, but he did agree about the wounding of Mangas Coloradas.

5. Daniel Ellis Conner. *Joseph Redford Walker and the Arizona Adventure.* Norman: The University of Oklahoma Press. 1956. The author's Apache informants always emphasized that mutilation of captives of the Apaches occurred only after death.

6. Individuals questioned the general Apache belief in Jeffords' honesty. Daklugie, for example, said that Jeffords ran contraband for Juh.

WITCHCRAFT (pp. 54-60)

1. Moses Loco, grandson of the chief, said his grandfather's eye was not damaged, but the face was so badly scarred that observers assumed there was no vision in the one eye.

WARPATH (pp. 61-70)

1. This account is almost identical with the report of Paul Blazer.

2. Nana knew that water from the spring (now known to be heavy in mineral salts) was very laxative. He surmised correctly that the cavalry would not know its properties and would use it for both men and horses, rendering them temporarily incapable of travel.

WANDERINGS (pp. 79-87)

1. Dan L. Thrapp. *Conquest of Apachería*. Norman: University of Oklahoma Press, 1967. The author referred to Mr. Thrapp's excellent book here and elsewhere to check and double-check certain aspects of this story.

TRES CASTILLOS (pp. 88-99)

1. The author is aware that this report of the massacre differs radically from the story as told in at least two other books: *Apache Days and After* by General Thomas Cruse (Caldwell, Idaho: Caxton Press, 1941) and *The Romance of the Davis Mountains and Big Bend Country* (El Paso: Rahtbooks, 1919). The account given here is that of Kaywaykla and Daklugie who both expressed distrust of the validity of the accounts from Cruse and Raht.

THE SURVIVORS (pp. 100-106)

1. It should be noted that the entire Tres Castillos episode and its aftermath in this chapter have been narrated from the childhood memories of James Kaywaykla, whose recollections were modified by hearing endless retelling of the episode from members of his family and friends.

MY UNCLES (pp. 107-114)

1. *Indah* was used by the Apaches to mean "white man," but literally translated it means "the living," as opposed to *Indeh,* used to mean "Apache," and literally translated as "dead."

2. Smugglers were said to walk usually a quarter of a mile or so behind the mule train to avoid sudden capture.

3. Daklugie and Istee, a son of Victorio, also told the author about the retreat in the barrancas and their recollections of having stayed there.

LOZEN (pp. 115-120)

1. Kaywaykla was mistaken. Lozen returned to the Mescalero Reservation and later married Calvin Zhunne. She was buried at White Tail.

CASAS GRANDES (pp. 129-135)

1. Father Albert Braun, in a 1965 interview at Mescalero, told the author that accounts describing *tiswin* as an intoxicant are exaggerated. He said that it was fermented rather than distilled, and furthermore, that the Indians seldom had enough corn, apart from needed food, to make a large quantity.

2. Without exception, all of the author's Apache informants insisted that their people would have preferred death to any form of captivity.

3. Jason Betzinez in *I Fought With Geronimo* (Harrisburg, Pa.: Stackpole, 1959) describes (with variations) this attack on the Mexicans, pp. 93-96.

LOCO (pp. 136-145)

1. Washington, D.C., *Daily Morning Chronicle,* November 10, 1872, pp. 1, 4 carried "A Report on General O. O. Howard's Mission to the Indians, and Peace Policy."

2. There was further reason for the stop-over. The author was told that one of the young girls had reached maturity and the Apaches believed that regardless of danger, the puberty rites must be performed.

3. The accounts of Betzinez and General Forsythe differ widely from that of Kaywaykla, who included these writers among the ones he did not trust.

FORT APACHE (pp. 146-153)

1. There are stories told as to the boy's death. Ruey Darrow, daughter of Sam Haouser, told the author in an interview that her family had taken the boy but that he was wounded by a stray bullet and died during the escape. Frank Lockwood in *The Apache Indians* (New York: Macmillan, 1938) also described the escape and the death of the boy.

2. Juh had made arrangements for securing ammunition at Casas Grandes.

3. Kaywaykla's narrative is here composited with that of Jasper Kanseah, youngest of the warriors, who died in the 1960s on the Mescalero Reservation. Lieutenant Britton Davis in *The Truth About Geronimo* (Reprinted, New Haven: Yale University Press, 1929) gives a similar account.

TURKEY CREEK (pp. 154-161)

1. Thrapp. *Op Cit.*

KAYTENNAE (pp. 162-167)

1. Chihuahua could understand much of what was said in English, and could speak a little English as well.

THE RETURN OF THE WOMEN (pp. 168-174)

1. Huera (whose name was the Spanish equivalent of "Blondie") was one of the women.

2. Cruse. *Op Cit.*

3. This account was given to the author in an interview with James Kaywaykla and Theodore Sedillo at Sedillo's home in Monticello.

THE OUTBREAK (pp. 175-180)

1. Davis. *Op Cit.*

2. Daklugie and Kaywaykla agreed that no Apache drank more than most of the white officers they knew.

3. John G. Bourke. *On the Border With Crook,* New York: Charles Scribner's Sons, 1891.

4. *Ibid.*

5. The author's interviews over a period of two decades with Eugene Chihuahua and his wife, Ramona, on the Mescalero Reservation.

SURRENDER (pp. 181-189)

1. Military reports such as that from Lieut. Britton Davis do not coincide with Kanseah's account as to the cause of the injury.

2. Ace Daklugie was a member of the group with Mangus.

3. Interviews by the author over a period of years with George Martine, son of Scout Martine, on the Mescalero Reservation.

4. Bourke. *Op Cit.*

5. This is speculation on the part of Kaywaykla.

GENERAL MILES (pp. 190-194)

1. Thrapp. *Op Cit.*
2. General Parker, U.S. Cavalry brevet brigadier general, later became Commissioner of Indian Affairs.

FLORIDA (pp. 195-204)

1. Although General Miles reported that Massai escaped from the train which carried Geronimo, the Apaches interviewed by the author insisted that he was on another train, the one carrying Kaywaykla.
2. Interview with Jasper Kanseah, and letter from Albert Wratten (son of George Wratten) to Eve Ball.
3. Kaywaykla was eight or nine years old when he was sent to Carlisle.
4. Chapo died of tuberculosis in Florida, according to Daklugie and Kaywaykla.
5. General George Crook. *Autobiography.* Ed. Martin Schnett. Norman: University of Oklahoma Press, 1960.
6. Members of the committee were James Kaywaykla, Jason Betzinez, Eugene Chihuahua, Robert Gooday, and Major Good.

Bibliography

BOOKS

BANCROFT, HUBERT HOWE. *The Works of Hubert Howe Bancroft.* Vol. 17. San Francisco: History Company, 1889.

BARRETT, G. M. *Geronimo's Story of His Life.* Interpreted by Ace Daklugie. New York: Nuffield & Co., 1906.

BASSO, KEITH H. *Western Apache Witchcraft. Anthropological Papers. No. 15.* Tucson: University of Arizona Press, 1969.

BENNETT, JAMES A. *Forts and Forays: The Diary of a Dragoon in New Mexico, 1850-1856.* Edited by Clinton Brooks and Frank Reeve. Albuquerque: University of New Mexico Press, 1948.

BETZINEZ, JASON, AND NYE, WILBUR S. *I Fought with Geronimo.* Harrisburg, Pa.: Stackpole Co., 1959.

BOURKE, CAPTAIN JOHN G. *On the Border with Crook.* New York: Scribner, 1891.

————. *An Apache Campaign in the Sierra Madre.* New York: Scribner, 1958.

————. *With General Crook in the Indian Wars.* Palo Alto, Calif.: Lewis Osbourne, 1968.

BRANDES, RAYMOND S. *Frontier Military Posts of Arizona.* Globe, Ariz.: Dale Stuart King, 1960.

BROOKS, CLINTON, and FRANK REEVE. *Forts and Forays.* Albuquerque: University of New Mexico Press, 1948.

BROWNE, JOHN ROSS. *Adventures in the Apache Country: A Tour through Arizona and Sonora.* New York: Harper & Bros., 1869.

CLUM, WOODWORTH. *Apache Agent.* New York: Houghton Mifflin Co., 1936.

COAN, CHARLES F. *A History of New Mexico.* 3 vols. Chicago: American Historical Society, 1925.

[211]

CONNER, DANIEL ELLIS. *Joseph Reddeford Walker and the Arizona Adventure.* Edited by Donald J. Berthrong and Odessa Davenport. Norman: University of Oklahoma Press, 1956.

COOKE, PHILIP ST. GEORGE. *The Conquest of New Mexico and California, 1846-1848.* Reprinted. Albuquerque: Horn and Wallace, 1964.

CORLE, EDWIN. *Desert Country.* New York: Duell, Sloan & Pearce, 1941.

CREMONY, JOHN C. *Life Among the Apaches.* (reprint) Tucson: Arizona Silhouettes, 1951.

CROCCHIOLA, STANLEY FRANCIS LOUIS. *The Apaches of New Mexico, 1514-1940.* Pampa, Texas: Pampa Print Shop, 1962.

————. *Fort Stanton, New Mexico.* Pampa, Texas: Pampa Print Shop, 1964.

CROOK, GENERAL GEORGE. *General George Crook: His Autobiography.* Edited and annotated by Martin F. Schmitt. Norman: University of Oklahoma Press, 1946.

CRUSE, GENERAL THOMAS. *Apache Days and After.* Edited by Eugene Cunningham. Caldwell, Idaho: Caxton Printers, Ltd., 1941.

CUMMINGS, BYRON. *Indians I Have Known.* Tucson: Arizona Silhouettes, 1952.

DALE, EDWARD EVERETT. *The Indians of the Southwest.* Norman: University of Oklahoma Press, 1949.

DAVIS, LIEUTENANT BRITTON. *The Truth about Geronimo.* Edited by M. M. Quaife. New Haven: Yale University Press, 1929. (This is considered by the Apaches to be authentic.)

DOBIE, J. FRANK. *Apache Gold and Yaqui Silver.* New York: Little, Brown & Co., 1939.

DUNN, JACOB PIATT, JR. *Massacres of the Mountains: A History of the Indian Wars of the Far West, 1815-1875.* New York: Harper & Bros., 1886.

EMORY, LIEUTENANT WILLIAM H. *Lieutenant Emory Reports.* Albuquerque: University of New Mexico Press, 1951.

FORSYTH, GENERAL GEORGE A. *Thrilling Days in Army Life.* New York: Harper & Bros., 1900.

FULTON, MAURICE GARLAND. *History of the Lincoln County War.* Edited by Robert N. Mullin. Tucson: University of Arizona Press, 1965.

GOODWIN, GRENVILLE. *Social Organization of the Western Apache.* Tucson: University of Arizona Press, 1969.

GREGG, JOSIAH. *Commerce of the Prairies.* (reprint) Dallas: Southwest Press, 1933.

GUITERAS, EUSEBIO, trans. *Rudo Ensayo: Arizona and Sonora, 1763.* Tucson: Arizona Silhouettes, 1951.

HAYES, JESS G. *Apache Vengeance.* Albuquerque: University of New Mexico Press, 1954.

HEITMAN, F. B. *Historical Reports and Dictionary of the U.S. Army From Its Organization, September 29, 1789, to March 2, 1903.* Facsimile Reprint, 2 vols. Urbana: University of Illinois Press, 1965.

History of New Mexico: Its Resources and People. New York: Pacific States Publishing Co., 1907.

HODGE, FREDERICK W. *Handbook of American Indians North of Mexico.* 2 vols. Washington, D.C.: Government Printing Office, 1912.

HOIJER, HARRY. *Chiricahua and Mescalero Apache Texts.* Chicago: University of Chicago Press, 1938.

HUGHES, JOHN T. *Doniphan's Expedition.* Cincinnati: J. A. & U. P. James, 1850.

JAMES, GEORGE WHARTON. *Indians of the Painted Desert.* New York: Little, Brown & Co., 1902.

KELEHER, WILLIAM A. *Turmoil in New Mexico, 1846-1868.* Santa Fe: Rydal Press, 1952.

————. *Violence in Lincoln County, 1869-1881.* Albuquerque: University of New Mexico Press, 1967.

KENDALL, GEORGE WILKINS. *Narrative of the Texan Santa Fe Expedition.* 2 vols. New York: Harper & Bros., 1844.

LECKIE, WILLIAM H. *The Buffalo Soldiers: A Narrative of Negro Cavalry in the West.* Norman: University of Oklahoma Press, 1967.

LOCKWOOD, FRANK C. *The Apache Indians.* New York: Macmillan Co., 1938.

LUMMIS, CHARLES F. *The Land of Poco Tiempo.* New York: Scribner, 1893.

MCKENNA, JAMES A. *Black Range Tales.* New York: Wilson-Erickson, Inc., 1936.

MAZZANOVICH, ANTON. *Trailing Geronimo.* Edited by E. A. Brininstool. Los Angeles: Gem Publishing Co., 1926. (The Apaches consider this unauthentic.)

MELTON, A. B. *Seventy Years in the Saddle and Then Some.* Kansas City Mo.: Cole Printing Service, 1950.

MILES, GENERAL NELSON A. *Personal Recollections and Observations.* Chicago: Werner Co., 1896.

OGLE, RALPH H. *Federal Control of the Western Apaches, 1846-1886.* Albuquerque: University of New Mexico Press, 1940.

OPLER, MORRIS E. *An Apache Life-way: The Economic, Social and Religious Institutions of the Chiricahua Indians.* Chicago: University of Chicago Press, 1941.

RAHT, CARLYSLE GRAHAM. *The Romance of Davis Mountains and Big Bend Country: A History.* El Paso, Texas: Rahtbooks Co., 1919.

Report of the Joint Special Committee. *Condition of the Indian Tribes.* Washington, D.C.: Government Printing Office, 1867.

RINGGOLD, JENNIE PARKS. *Frontier Days in the Southwest.* San Antonio, Texas: Naylor Co., 1952.

RISTER, CARL COKE. *The Southwestern Frontier — 1865-1881.* Cleveland, Ohio: Arthur H. Clark Co., 1928.

SABIN, EDWIN L. *Kit Carson Days, 1809-1868.* Chicago: A. G. McClure & Co., 1914.

SEDELMAYR, JACOBO. *Jacobo Sedelmayr: Missionary, Frontiersman, Explorer in Arizona and Sonora.* 4 original manuscript narratives, 1744-1751. Translated and annotated by Peter Masten Dunne. Tucson: Arizona Pioneers' Historical Society, 1955.

SHINKLE, JAMES D. *Fort Sumner and the Bosque Redondo Indian Reservation.* Roswell, N.M.: Hall-Poorbaugh Press, 1965.

SMITH, CORNELIUS C., JR. *William Sanders Oury: History-Maker of the Southwest.* Tucson: University of Arizona Press, 1967.

SONNICHSEN, C. L. *The Mescalero Apaches.* Norman: University of Oklahoma Press, 1958.

214   BIBLIOGRAPHY

THRAPP, DAN L. *The Conquest of Apachería.* Norman: University of Oklahoma Press, 1967.
————. *Al Sieber, Chief of Scouts.* Norman: University of Oklahoma Press, 1964.
TWITCHELL, RALPH K. *The Leading Facts of New Mexican History.* 2 vols. Cedar Rapids, Ia.: Torch Press, 1911-1912.
WALKER, HENRY PICKERING. *The Wagonmasters.* Norman: University of Oklahoma Press, 1966.
WARFIELD, COL. H. B. (USAF, Rt.) *Apache Indian Scouts.* El Cajon, California: Privately printed, 1964.
WEBB, WALTER PRESCOTT. *The Great Plains.* Boston: Ginn & Co., 1931.
WELLMAN, PAUL I. *Death in the Desert.* New York: Macmillan Co., 1935.
WELSH, HERBERT. *The Apache Prisoners in Fort Marion, St. Augustine, Florida.* Philadelphia: Office of the Indian Rights Association, 1887.
WHIPPLE, LIEUTENANT AMIEL W. *Report upon the Indian Tribes.* Vol. 3. Washington, D.C.: 1855.
WILLIAMS, OSCAR WALDO. *The Personal Narrative of O. W. Williams: Pioneer Surveyor, Frontier Lawyer.* Edited by S. D. Myers. El Paso: Texas Western College Press, 1966.
WISSLER, CLARK. *Indians of the United States: Four Centuries of Their History.* New York: Doubleday, Doran & Co., Inc., 1940.

ARTICLES

BLAZER, ALMER N. "Beginnings of an Indian War." *New Mexico Magazine* 16 (1938): 22.
CLUM, WOODWORTH. "The Apaches." *New Mexico Historical Review* 4 (1929): 107-127.
HUMPHRIES, KEITH. "Trail of the Pioneers." *New Mexico Magazine* 17 (1939): 10.
LYON, JUAN FRAZER. *An Apache Brand of Clan McIntosh Clan Chatten.* Vol. IV No. 2. January, 1961.
OPLER, MORRIS E. "A Chiricahua Apache's Account of the Geronimo Campaign of 1886, by Samuel Kenoi." *New Mexico Historical Review* 13 (1938): 360-386.
REEVE, FRANK D. "The Federal Policy in New Mexico, 1858-1880." *New Mexico Historical Review* 13 (1938): I, 14-62; II, 146-191; III, 261-313.
THOMPKINS, WALTER ALLISON. "Bowie: Guardian of Apache Pass," *Arizona Highways,* March, 1958.

MANUSCRIPTS AND DOCUMENTS

BLAZER, ALMER N. "Santana, the Last Chief of the Mescaleros." Unpublished manuscript, courtesy of Paul Blazer.
Bureau of American Ethnology. *Handbook of American Indians.* Edited by Frederick Webb Hodge. Bulletin 80, Part 1. Washington, D.C.: Government Printing Office, 1907.
Executive Orders, 1871, 1874, and 1877 affecting Apaches.

Museum of Missiles and Artillery, Fort Sill, Okla., Gillett Griswold, Curator. Cemetery Roll of Apaches Buried at Fort Sill.

THOMPSON, JAMES. Record made from Stenographic Notes on Decision of Chiricahua and Warm Springs Apaches as to Leaving Fort Sill.

————. A Report on the Number of Apaches Going to the Mescalero Apache Reservation, and their Assets.

INTERVIEWS

BARTON, DEL (MRS. ROBERT). Great granddaughter of Grey Wolf, Seneca chief. At Ruidoso, sometimes with Eugene and Jennie Chihuahua, her adoptive parents by Apache custom.

BEGAY, ALBERTA. Daughter of Massai; married to a Navajo. Interviews both at her home and mine in 1959, 1960, and 1961.

BIG MOUTH. Before his death, the only surviving Apache scout. Frequent interviews in 1946, with his son interpreting. Big Mouth lived to be more than a hundred, having been a scout for the Seventh Cavalry and for cavalry stationed at Fort Sill.

BLAZER, PAUL. Grandson of Dr. Joseph Blazer, dentist who owned the mill which was surrounded by the Apache reservation. Information was given over a period of fifteen years.

BRAUN, FATHER ALBERT. Interviews at Mescalero, July, 1967, 1968.

CHAVEZ, ABEL AND TEODOLO. Aged Spanish-Americans; interviews with James Kaywaykla present at their home in Monticello and on November 23, 1953.

CHAVEZ, CARLOS. Interview at State House, Chihuahua, Chihuahua, Mexico with James Kaywaykla, Dr. Kathleen Doering, and Mrs. Zoe Glasmire present.

CHIHUAHUA, EUGENE. Son of Chief Chihuahua, Chiricahua chief. Numerous interviews over a period of twelve years.

CHIHUAHUA, JENNIE. Wife of Chief Chihuahua. Her father was a Mexican boy captured by Navajos, sold into slavery, and finally rescued by Apaches. Because he knew Spanish, English, and Apache he became the interpreter on the Mescalero Apache Reservation.

COJO, GLADYS SCOTT (Apache). Interview at Ruidoso, September, 1960.

COONIE, ELIZA. Sister of Hugh Coonie; numerous interviews over many years.

COONIE, HUGH. Son of scout Coonie; numerous interviews over a period of twenty years at my home.

DAHTESTE. Stepmother of Hugh and Eliza Coonie; she spoke no English and they interpreted. Interviews in my home in 1946 and 1947.

DAKLUGIE, ACE. Son of the Nednhi chief, Juh; husband of Ramona, sister to Eugene Chihuahua. He spent one day each week for many months dictating his experiences.

ENJADY, ISABEL PERICO (Mrs. Clarence Enjady). Numerous interviews at her home at Whitetail and at mine in Ruidoso.

FATTY, EUSTACE. Son of Old Fatty, leader of a Warm Springs band. Numerous interviews.

GALLARITO, CARRIZO (Crook Neck). He lived to be over a hundred; went to Mexico with Victorio; was born (he thought) in 1853. He was one of the few who spoke no English, and his son, John Gallarito, interpreted.

GERONIMO, MAUDE DAKLUGIE. Daughter-in-law of Geronimo. Numerous interviews at Ruidoso and Carisso.

GERONIMO, ROBERT. Son of Geronimo. Many interviews at Apache Summit.

ISTEE, CHARLES. Son of Victorio. Numerous interviews at Whitetail, his home. As long as he lived he anticipated that because he was Victorio's son he might be killed by white people.

ISTEE, EVANS. Son of Charles Istee. Numerous interviews.

JONES, SAM, BILL, FRANK, AND NIB. Over a period of years both in their homes and mine.

JOZHE, BENEDICT. At Ruidoso, July 7, 1959, and at other times.

KANSEAH, JASPER. Nephew of Geronimo and his youngest warrior. Many interviews in 1953-1959 in which he recounted his experiences on the warpath with Geronimo.

KAYITAH, KENNETH. Grandson of the scout who went with Martine to Geronimo.

KAYWAYKLA, JAMES. Nephew of Victorio and grandnephew of Nana; innumerable interviews over a period of seven years.

KENOI, SAM. Son of Fatty, whom the Mexicans called Gordo. Interviews at Mescalero and in my home.

LOCO, MOSES. Grandson of Chief Loco; interview October 6, 1959, primarily concerning his grandfather.

MAGOOSH, WILLIE. Son of Lipan chief who brought his people to the Mescalero Apache Reservation for refuge; interviews in July, 1947, and in 1948 and 1949.

MAGOOSH, WYNONA. Daughter of Yanosha, one of Geronimo's warriors.

MAHILL, FRANK. Interviews at Mayhill, New Mexico, in 1951.

MARTINE, GEORGE. Son of the famous scout who went to Geronimo's camp and with Kayitah, induced the Bedonkohe leader to meet with the cavalry.

NICHOLAS, DAN. Son of the famous Chiricahua runner, Nicholas. Mastered the international code of phonetics and put the Apache language into print. He also collected and wrote the coyote legends, planning at the time of his death in March, 1969, to put the legends of his people into book form.

PESO, ALTON. Son of Mescalero Chief Peso; numerous interviews in 1954 and 1955.

PESO, LUCIUS. Son of Chief Peso; three interviews in June, 1950.

SECOND, MAY PESO. Daughter of Chief Peso; many interviews both in my home and at Mescalero.

SEDILLO, SIXTO. Aged Spanish-American; interview at his home on the Rio Ruidoso in 1947.

SEDILLO, THEODORE. Interview at Monticello, New Mexico, on November 23, 1953.

SHANTA, LYDIA DAKLUGIE (Mrs. Ralph). Interviews at my home in 1950-1953.

SHANTA, RALPH. Son-in-law of Daklugie; numerous interviews over a period of years.

SMITH, CHARLIE. Mescalero, aged about 93; interviews at his home in White Tail and at mine in Ruidoso. His mother had been captured by one of Geronimo's warriors, who took her and her son, Charlie, on the warpath with Geronimo for three years.

SOMBRERO, SOLON. A leader among his people; grandson of Natzili (Buffalo chief of the Mescaleros). Many interviews.

VENEGO, PHILEMON (Lipan Apache). He was a small child when the Lipans contracted smallpox near San Antonio and divided into small groups. His went to Mexico and lived near Zaragosa until James A. Carroll, agent at Mescalero, sent Father Migeon, parish priest at Tularosa, to bring them to the reservation where their tribe, under Chief Magoosh, had taken refuge many years earlier. Many interviews over a number of years.

WILSON, WOODROW. Succeeded his father, Elmer Wilson, as Mescalero Apache medicine man. Many interviews both on the reservation and in Ruidoso.

LETTERS

ACEVES, JOSE. To Eve Ball, June 28, 1961.

Apache Agents. To Commissioner of Indian Affairs, during the administrations with which the book is concerned.

BARTON, MRS. DEL. Numerous letters regarding the Apaches.

CLUM, JOHN. To John Wasson, April 31, 1877, from the Southern Apache Agency; published in the *Arizona Citizen* of Tucson.

FULTON, MAURICE GARLAND. Numerous letters to Eve Ball over a period of several years.

JOZHE, BENEDICT. To Eve Ball, July 10, 1963.

LOCO, MOSES. To Eve Ball, August 15, 1963.

WRATTEN, ALBERT. To Eve Ball, regarding article published September 10, 1961.

Index

IN THE DAYS OF VICTORIO

Recollections of a Warm Springs Apache

by EVE BALL

JAMES KAYWAYKLA, *Narrator*

"Until I was about ten years old I didn't know that people died except by violence."

With these arresting words, Kaywaykla, descendant of Chief Victorio, begins the story of the first turbulent decade of his childhood, coinciding with the climactic years of flight, pursuit, and final capture of the Apache people.

Through this vivid, accurate recall, the reader will experience the desperation of Apache families — men, women, children, the aged — driven by "fire and sword" from their homeland, herded onto various reservations, chased back and forth across the Mexican border, promised, tricked, finally maneuvered in defeat and weariness aboard the trains that took them in 1886 to Florida prisons for further confinement.

Major figures — also relatives and friends — in the drama that raged around the child Kaywaykla were Chief Victorio himself as well as other Apache notables — Loco, Chihuahua, and Kaywaykla's great-uncle Nana; the warrior woman, Lozen, and the always rebellious Geronimo.

In the breathing spaces Kaywaykla reveals also the more humane texture of Apache daily life: the affectionate families,